FOR WHAT IT'S WORTH

FOR WHAT IT'S WORTH

BUSINESS WISDOM FROM A PAWNBROKER

LES GOLD

Portfolio / Penguin

PORTFOLIO / PENGUIN
Published by the Penguin Group
Penguin Group (USA) Inc., 375 Hudson Street,
New York, New York 10014, USA

USA / Canada / UK / Ireland / Australia / New Zealand / India / South
Africa / China

Penguin Books Ltd, Registered Offices: 80 Strand,
London WC2R 0RL, England
For more information about the Penguin Group visit penguin.com

PHOTOGRAPH CREDITS
Insert page 4 (top), 5 (middle and bottom), 6 (bottom left and right),
7 (top left),
8 (top left and right): Robert "Bobby J" Janiec
Page 4 (bottom), 5 (top), 6 (top), 7 (top right and bottom): Randy Smith
Other photographs courtesy of the author

ISBN 978-1-59184-639-0

Printed in the United States of America
1   3   5   7   9   10   8   6   4   2

Book design by Neuwirth & Associates, Inc.

To my beautiful wife, Lili:

If it were not for you, I do not know where I would be today—certainly not writing this book.

You are my inspiration to get up every single day and do what I do.

You have been pushing me to live up to my potential each incredible step of this journey.

I love you, babe.

CONTENTS

FOR WHAT IT'S WORTH

Introduction

I am lucky enough to have an unusual job. Well, that's putting it mildly. My business, pawnbroking, goes in so many directions, there's no such thing as a typical day at work. One day, I might be taking in a 1965 Bentley in pawn. The next, I might be running out into the street after someone who's just lifted a gold chain. I've been a master negotiator, a jeweler, a gun salesman, a car dealer, a confidant to the down on their luck, a gambler, and a loyal citizen of Detroit. Dealing with the unexpected is one of the reasons I became a pawnbroker—and learning to love the craziness is one of the reasons I'm so damn good at it.

While I've been the star of *Hardcore Pawn*, you may have seen me try to make deals for a hearse and a stripper pole and an Olympic torch. You've seen me deal with customers who start fights, an employee who bit a colleague, and a trusted manager who turned out to be a thief. You've seen me fight with my son, Seth, and my daughter, Ashley—my best, or at least my loudest, employees—and you've seen our relationship evolve every day as we work together. You've gotten a sense of what life is like in our crazy little slice of Detroit.

My job isn't easy, but I love what I do—and that passion helps me succeed. I first opened my shop, American Jewelry and Loan, in a tiny fifteen-hundred-square-foot space in a strip mall. Now we've expanded into a fifty-thousand-square-foot former bowling alley. I started out making two or three loans a day. Now we make a thousand loans a day and employ fifty-five people.

In more than five decades of pawnbroking, I've learned invaluable business lessons I couldn't have learned anywhere else. No business school in the world could have taught me everything I learned in pawnshops: buying, selling, negotiating, managing employees, dealing with customers, advertising, tracking trends in technology and fashion, and predicting the economy's ups and downs. Doing my job well takes determination, courage, and love. In this book I'm going to share what I've learned from fifty-five years in the most interesting job in the world.

Whether you're a fellow pawnbroker, the owner of a small business, a manager trying to work as hard as possible to get the best from your employees, or an individual trying to build a career you'll love, I believe I can offer you valuable lessons learned across a lifetime in business. I not only practice what I preach, but I also constantly try to change the perception of what it takes to be successful. If I can make a splash across the country by running the best pawnshop possible, I believe that all people have opportunities to better themselves through their careers.

One reason I wanted to write this book is that throughout my career—throughout my life—I've been trying to change the ideas people have about pawnshops. If you walk into a traditional pawnshop in China, the pawnbroker is sitting above you. The very arrangement is telling you you're no good; it's demeaning to walk into that store. Today, pawnshops may be laid out differently, but too often the message is still the same: This is a place that caters to desperate people who need money for food, rent, and car payments, money to keep life going.

When I look at my store, American Jewelry and Loan, I see something different. I see a dynamic business that can adapt to any kind of economic environment. I see an exciting enterprise that's constantly changing and constantly surprising me. I see a retail center that's a resource for the Detroit communities I live and work in. I see the hundreds of people I've helped over the years. I see the lessons I learned working in my grandfather's pawnshop and the legacy I'm trying to leave for my kids.

Over the years I've made lots of changes to my pawnshop, but they've all been in service to this higher purpose: building a business I can be proud to leave to my children. I don't want to leave my kids a business that looks down on its customers. At the shop, we make sure it's not demeaning to pawn something with us. When you walk into my store and you see a hundred people in line behind you, you know you can feel good about what you're doing.

My grandfather Popsie immigrated to America in 1905 when he was twelve. To help his family financially he became a rag picker in the United States, driving his horse and buggy around looking for junk on the side of the road that he could sell. In the 1940s, with my great-grandfather, he opened a pawnshop. Today, the grandson of a onetime rag picker and the son of a sometime pool hustler, I'm running a million-dollar business and starring in a reality TV show. It's amazing what you can do in this country if you're willing to work hard and smart. America was built by entrepreneurs, and it still rewards those who have the initiative, drive, and commitment to build something new.

It's taken me a long time to build a business I can be proud of. In this book I'm going to show you how I did it. I'm going to reveal how I took my family's business on this journey from literal rags to riches. What's more, I'm going to tell you the secrets of my success: I'm going to teach you to think like a pawnbroker. A pawnbroker knows the value of everything, from a fur coat to a person's word of honor. In this book I'll teach you how you, too, can learn to get what you need for what it's worth, in the broad sense.

In some ways I'm already a teacher. People come up to me on the street all the time and tell me that they learned to negotiate from watching *Hardcore Pawn*. I've met all kinds of viewers, from businessmen in suits to young vets who just got back from Afghanistan to ex-cons (apparently, I'm a big hit in the joint). They tell me how important my show is to them, and how they've learned about deal making by watching me operate.

Sometimes people even ask me to negotiate for them. I was out in California in June 2012 with my wife, Lili, and some friends of ours, and we were all wandering around an art fair. My friends spotted a big painting of a tiger by a Chinese artist and instantly knew they wanted to buy it. They wanted me to negotiate the deal for them. The seller was asking for $3,200; my friends said they wanted to pay $1,600. The seller insisted that, at such a low price, he couldn't possibly include the book about the artist's work that he usually gives all his customers. I played hardball with the price and told him we didn't need the book. We negotiated and settled on $2,100 for the painting—book included.

Another couple was standing nearby and watched me make the deal. When I was done helping out my friend, the woman in the couple asked, "Can you do that for me, too?"

Here's the thing: I love negotiating. I love making deals. Most people hate it, and that's why they're no good at it. They want to get it over with more than they want to get a good deal. At the art fair, the woman who asked me for help said she'd pay $600 for a small piece. I told her, "No, you won't." I got her the art for $400, plus that book—and, of course, she got a master class in negotiation.

The notion that I'm sort of a teacher is a strange feeling, because I never liked school. I always wanted to get back to the pawnshop and back to selling alongside my grandfather. I might have been an average student, but I was a great salesman—and I didn't learn in any fancy MBA program. My grandfather's pawnshop was my business school, and I wouldn't trade the education I got there for any Ivy League degree. Everything I learned there I learned by doing. No textbook teaches the lessons as well as the school of life does.

I learned how to make a sale by jumping in and selling. I learned to love being surprised by the strange things people would bring into the store. I learned to build a business that would always grow and change. I learned the importance of making my customers believe they could trust me to give them a fair deal. And most of all, I learned to take care of family first, even when they were the ones letting me down.

In this book I'm going to teach you the philosophy and practice that will help you run a successful business.

The very first lesson I learned was that in order to be successful, you've got to be able to face your fears. Everyone, in every business, is afraid of something: You may be scared about your job security, intimidated by your boss, even physically threatened! I've been all three. In Chapter 1, I'll take you through my early years working for my toughest boss ever—my father. My fear of becoming the failure he always told me I'd be held me back. It wasn't until I learned to believe in myself (with some help from my beloved grandfather Popsie) that I was really able to trust my own instincts and business sense. Chapter 2 will help you figure out how to act like a champion and find your inner ally, just like Popsie helped me do.

I believe the most important factor in succeeding in business is to love what you do. Real joy at work, as we'll explore in Chapter 3, is what gets you up every day. Maybe you don't have the opportunity to work at a place that constantly changes, the way that American Jewelry and Loan does. But I guarantee you can find something to love about your job and you can find some way to change it for the better. In Chapter 4, I'll explain why I believe you need to have a no-boundaries, anything-goes attitude toward your business or your career. You can't let yourself or your business be limited by what you've done before, what everybody else is doing, or what conventional wisdom says you should do.

It's not all about attitude; I'm also going to teach you some hard skills that are useful in any business, in any industry. In Chapter 5, we'll look at how to negotiate like a pawnbroker. I'll explain the role of emotion in buying and selling, and show you how to use it to your advantage. You'll learn the way I learned, from watching a master pawnbroker at work. In Chapter 6, I'll talk about some of the key questions you need to answer before starting a new business. From the best way to manage employees to the surefire best way to win your boss's heart, I'll reveal the reality of long-term success and show you how to handle setbacks and pay the price of success.

Whether you own your own business or whether you're just starting out, your reputation is all you have. In Chapter 7, I'll show you how to build a reputation for being reliable and trustworthy by deserving that reputation every day, in everything you do. As a pawnbroker, this is a little harder for me than for many business owners because the industry I work in has a shady reputation. But I believe businesspeople who want to be successful need to be thinking about their legacy with every decision they make. In Chapter 8, you'll see why it's so important to me to leave behind a legacy that my children will be proud of. My whole career has been fueled by love and explains why I think any successful business needs to begin with love as a foundation.

In this book, you'll see that I'm not just running a family business; I'm running a business where everyone is like family. My core employees are part of my family now. We celebrate holidays together. Although I may not be quite as close with all fifty of my employees, I do try to create a family atmosphere for the entire business. I watched Popsie bring in hot dogs for the troops every Saturday when I was a kid, and now I hold potluck lunches for the staff in December, when the retail side of our business is particularly busy and everyone is working long hours. I believe those personal bonds help make my business more successful.

I'm building a business meant to last for generations, not just to be successful today. I'm building a legacy and a whole new approach to doing business the right way. In this book we'll go behind the scenes of *Hardcore Pawn*. You'll see what running a pawnshop is really like when the cameras aren't rolling, and you'll hear the whole story of my life. You'll get my master class in negotiation. Perhaps most important, you'll see where I've come from, and where I believe I'm going.

Desire for success is what binds me to you as you hold this book in your hands. I've been through extremely hard times to get to where I am—and I want you to believe you can be just as successful, by working hard and applying my principles of success to your work life. Every day of his life, my father told me I was never going to be good enough. But I wanted more than the narrow role he saw for me. I worked hard to prove him wrong. I made my first sale at seven. By the time I was thirteen, I was selling golf clubs out of my basement on the weekends. At thirty-one, I left my father behind to build my own business. Now I write a thousand loans a day, and my show, *Hardcore Pawn,* is the most successful show in truTV's history.

I believe you can have the same victory and thrill in your business or career. I made a choice to fight against what other people thought I should do and be—and I think you can, too. Let's get started on your journey of success.

[CHAPTER 1]

Face Your Fear

We all deal with fear, whether we are fully aware of it or not, and whether we acknowledge it or not. Certain fears start in childhood, with the parent or teacher or bully who tried to put us down or the sibling who tormented us. Then there are the everyday fears we face at work: *Can I make this sale? Will I get this promotion? Can I get through this presentation without embarrassing myself?* And, finally, there are the big life fears: *Am I safe? Will my business succeed? Will I be able to provide for my family?* In this chapter I'm going to show you how to master all those fears that are holding you back. You'll learn

+ **how to look your fear in the eye;**
+ **how to perform despite your fear;**
+ **how to accept your biggest fears; and**
+ **how to make your fear work for you.**

Growing Up with Fear

Fear was with me every day when I was growing up, thanks to my father. He was not a kind man. He was not even a nice one. He wouldn't let me call him Dad—he insisted that I call him L.G., at least in public. He didn't want anyone to know he had a son; that might have made him seem older than he wanted to be taken for.

I don't remember L.G. beating me, but I do know that he mentally abused me. Maybe he thought it would make me a better man. Maybe he just didn't know another way to be; his dad had treated him the same way. His dad broke his thumb once, just because L.G. didn't want to get out of bed one morning. But every day of my young life I had my dad's voice in my ear, telling me I was no good, that I'd never amount to anything, that I was stupid.

The pawnshop I grew up working in belonged to Popsie, who was my mother's father. It was a family business, and my mom used to work there sometimes. When Mom got pregnant with me and then married my dad, Popsie brought his new son-in-law into the business, too. My grandparents knew the kind of man my father was, but once I was born, L.G. was a part of the family. They felt they had no choice but to employ him so that he could support my mom, my sister, and me. Popsie even let our family live with him and my Bubbie for a couple years.

Impregnating my mom was a real stroke of luck for my dad. Before he met her, he had been a pool hustler and had worked in a refrigerator factory. But when my grandfather gave him a job at the pawnshop, L.G. had a chance at real success. He had a golden opportunity to learn from Popsie, a man who had worked his way up from nothing to build a solid business. Popsie started his business career driving a horse and buggy, picking up junk along the way, and reselling it to make money.

Popsie was bigger than life, and a genuine success. He had the drive, the courage, and the basic decency to succeed at anything he did. As an immigrant in the Midwest in the early twentieth century, there weren't a lot of options for people like him. He took to the pawnshop business the way he did everything: with enthusiasm. If he was going to be a pawnbroker, then he would be the best pawnbroker anywhere.

My dad didn't possess any of those sterling qualities. He wasn't cut out to be a salesman. He didn't much like going to work for my Popsie. He wasn't devoted to the business the way Popsie was and only cared about being a pawnbroker because of the money he could make. He didn't have a love of business; he had a love of the dollar. Deep down, I believe he never had much confidence in himself as a salesman or a businessman. So he did his best to instill the same lack of confidence in me.

He was a Golden Gloves boxer, and when I was younger, sometimes we would put on the gloves and play around. It's one of the few good memories I have of L.G. But I remember one time when we were sparring and suddenly I could see in his eyes that he wasn't kidding anymore. He started swinging for real. Luckily, I was still pretty young at the time, and I could move much faster than he could, or I don't know what would have happened. I just ran, terrified, right out of the house.

I honestly don't remember if he ever hit me without the gloves. I can remember him coming after me with a belt when I was in trouble. But I don't remember if he actually hit me. Maybe it's one of those things you block out of your mind. I do remember my mother trying to stand up for me when he berated me, but she was frightened of L.G., too. He verbally abused us both. He told her she was fat, she was ugly—anything to tear her down.

Even if he didn't hit me, my dad did plenty to mentally abuse me and destroy my self-worth. He did his best to convince me that I had an Oedipus complex and to make me as miserable as he was.

The Toll Fear Takes

It was a struggle just living in the same house with him. There were nights I would lie in bed and cry because of how he had made me feel. I think he was jealous of the close relationships I had with my grandparents and my mom. And when I started learning how to sell, he was jealous of that, too.

I made my first sale at the pawnshop when I was seven years old. A man came in wanting to buy a hydraulic jack. Popsie had brought me into the store with him that day—he did that at least once a week—and my dad was there, too. On that particular day, they told me to take the sale, on my own.

I was intimidated. I didn't even know what a hydraulic jack was. I was seven years old—all I knew about were crayons. But I started talking to the customer, and my dad and my Popsie walked over to stand behind him. They watched me and gave me hand signals. They told me to start at fifteen dollars, but the customer said he would only pay eight. I looked over at Popsie and he raised his thumb, indicating that I should try to go higher. I told the customer, "How about twelve dollars?" He responded, "How about ten?"

We settled on ten dollars. It felt like closing a million-dollar deal. It was the beginning of my infatuation with selling, but it was also the moment when my dad really became threatened by my skills. L.G. took his anger and frustration out on the family. He and my mom would fight all the time. I learned early to try to be the man of the house and would stick up for my mother, even with my father there. Of course, he'd get mad at me for doing that. I could never escape L.G. In the house or out of the house, it felt like I was always competing with him, a child against an adult. It felt like he didn't want to be my father at all.

When you're a kid, you think your parents love you automatically. But now I can see that my dad was constantly cutting me down because he wanted to keep me stuck in a little box of fear where he could control me. My father wanted me to fail. He was relying on me to help support the family, but he didn't want me to see myself as his equal. He wanted me to be subordinate to him.

When I was fourteen, my dad fell through a display case in the store and cut all the tendons in his foot. He had surgery and then required physical therapy for a while. Every night I had to be his physical therapist and sit with him and massage his foot. That was right where he wanted me—at his feet. Taking care of him. Making him feel big, even though I was only a little kid.

Again and again I learned how much he wanted to put me down. But I also learned that I could prove him wrong. I could face my fear and stand on an equal playing field with the grown-ups. After all, if I wasn't allowed to be his son, I could at least be his colleague.

I hope there's no one in your life who puts you down like my father did me. But if there is, you just have to learn to face the fear and the sick feeling in the pit of your stomach that goes with it.

Learn to Look Fear in the Eye

Because I wasn't allowed to be a kid, I learned pretty early to act like one of the adults. When I made my first sale at seven, I became hooked: on the exhilaration, the excitement, the feeling of accomplishment. It was overwhelming and I couldn't get enough of it. I was still a little kid, but I'd stood on the same level as an adult. I could be scared of my father and intimidated by him in all other ways, but I'd begun to realize that I had power of my own in the pawnshop.

I couldn't wait for the Saturdays when Popsie would take me to the pawnshop. I was scared the first time I had to negotiate with a customer, but with practice it got easier. I learned that I could sell. Gradually, Popsie let me learn more and then allowed me to try out all aspects of the business, from buying to selling and all the negotiating in between. And as I got older and L.G. tried harder and harder to teach me fear, the knowledge that I had these skills helped me not to believe him when he belittled me. I could look at myself and know that I wasn't an idiot after all.

When I was about twelve, we had a gold Timex watch in the window of Popsie's pawnshop. A woman came in and wanted to buy it, and after a bit of negotiating, I sold it to her for $20. My dad chewed me out in front of everyone in the store, including the customer, because he thought I should have held out for $25 for the watch. He humiliated his own son over a measly $5.

But I was learning to keep going in spite of him. OK, I went into the bathroom and cried. I was still a kid. But then I dried my tears and looked in the mirror and told myself that L.G. was wrong about me. I pulled myself together and I went back out into the store. L.G. pretended nothing had happened.

You can't get past your fears by avoiding them, any more than I could avoid my father's cruelty. The only thing you can do is learn to look your fear in the eye. Do it literally if you have to, the way I did after my dad yelled at me about the watch: Look at yourself in the mirror. It took a few years before I was ready to confront L.G. directly, but I was eventually able to do that, too, as you'll see.

You should acknowledge what's happening to you and that you're afraid that the person telling you you're nothing is right. But that person is *not* right. Every individual on this earth deserves respect. Every person has a chance to succeed, including you. Look your fear in the eye, see that your fear doesn't define your strengths . . . and then get back to work.

Face Your Fear—and Move On

It wasn't just my dad who was after me. I was also scared on my own account. I was afraid of the risks you have to take to get started in this big, bad world. I knew I wanted to be successful and prove L.G. wrong, but I was fearful of taking a chance on myself.

When I was fifteen, I started a new side business. I used to walk around department stores to see what was popular. It was my way of doing market research before we were able to Google anything. On my research trips, I noticed that chain vests, belts, and bracelets seemed to be selling. Well, I was good in shop class and I was good with my hands. I wouldn't necessarily call myself an artist, but I've always been quite creative. So I came up with a design for my own chain jewelry: bracelets, necklaces, and chains. I kept it simple.

My mother drove me to a hardware store where you could buy chain by the inch, and I bought the materials and started making demos for my own line of jewelry. I took my first items to little jewelry and clothing boutiques downtown. That wasn't so daunting; I would just walk into these places. Many were small and most of them were owned by women, so I wasn't quite as intimidated about going in to try to make a sale. I would sell about eight or ten pieces at a time to these small stores.

At first I didn't know how to price my chains. I knew how much it cost me to buy the materials and, of course, I wanted to make a profit. At the first couple of boutiques I went into, I just pulled a price out of the air—$20—but that was too high. The buyers said no. So I'd ask them, "Well, how much do you think you could sell it for?" They'd tell me and then I'd name a price below that figure, $10 or a little bit more.

I learned that a good salesperson has to be a good listener, and that was a great way to get over my fear. Once I started to understand the buyer, I was more comfortable with what I was doing, and the fear melted away. If you don't listen—if you do all the talking—you'll never get anywhere. You won't know what your product will bring unless you listen to your customer. If you're trying to sell something, it's easy to determine what it's worth:

It's worth what the market will pay for it, not what you think it's worth. Selling that first jewelry line, I quickly began to understand that those buyers knew the worth of their merchandise and that I could learn from their understanding of their business. Learning more of the business from their perspective helped me get past my ignorance and lowered my fear.

For a year and a half I continued to buy my material at the hardware store and sell my chains to the little boutiques. The products sold well, and I was constantly going back to the hardware store for more chain. The hardware store sold it only by the inch, but eventually, because I came in so often, the hardware seller told me about the manufacturer in California who could sell me chain by the yard. I could stock supplies more easily, increase my output, and cut down on expenses.

I knew that when I made the call to California, I couldn't sound like a kid. I had to project enough confidence that the manufacturer would believe I was running a real business. So when I called, I made sure to throw around words like "designer," "manufacturer," and "in-house." My tactic worked. Not only did they agree to sell me the chain, they also agreed to bill me for it later.

I didn't make a ton of money from selling jewelry, but I made enough to keep myself in spending money and saved a nice sum toward my first car. That was my goal: a car. It meant freedom from L.G. and freedom from fear.

By the time I was eighteen I was pretty confident about the jewelry business. But I wanted more. So I opened the Yellow Pages and looked up the number for J.L. Hudson's, an iconic Detroit department store. I called the main office and told them I was a sales rep for a company called Gold Associates and that I had a line of gold-plated jewelry I'd like to show the buyers. The operator transferred me to the jewelry department and I set up an appointment with their accessory buyer.

Talking to a huge department store over the phone was one thing. But for me to go in and meet with a real buyer in person—talk about scared! What if my mind went blank? What if I couldn't talk to this person the way I talked to the boutique owners I'd been working with? What if they didn't like the jewelry?

I knew I had to at least look professional. I borrowed a briefcase from the pawnshop to make myself a little display. Going into that big office, I could feel my heart beating fast as I opened up my case and showed my jewelry. It was the late sixties and all the secretaries in the office were women, so the buyer took my case and walked it around the office, showing it to the secretaries to see what they thought of the jewelry. I can't describe how scared I was while he was walking around. I could barely breathe, I was so nervous. But I knew I could not let them see the nervousness in my face and that I had to keep the smile on. The buyer finished showing my jewelry to the women and came back to me. "Take out your purchase order agreement," he said.

I was in. J.L. Hudson's bought $4,000 worth of my chains. They wanted them in thirty days. I was so glad to get the order that I made the chains and delivered them on time, working like crazy to get them done.

One of the most exciting moments in my life was the day I walked into that store and saw my chains for sale. Those were my first steps toward becoming a real professional. It felt like the big time to me, and I had done it on my own.

After my triumph with J.L. Hudson's, I went to every department store in town. The selling process got easier with every store I visited because now I knew what to expect. I knew how to react when I walked in and people would say, "You're just a kid; how do we know you'll follow through?" A buyer for a department store doesn't want to waste his time making an order if you're not going to fulfill it. They were looking for assurances and, luckily, I had the pawnshop experience behind me. I knew how to talk. I knew that as long as I didn't show any fear, I could look those people in the eye and make them believe in me. I also knew that if by chance I did make some mistake, like quoting the wrong price, I'd learn how to do better next time.

Performing Despite Your Fear

One of the most important lessons I learned when selling my jewelry was that I needed to *outperform* my fear. I had to act smarter and older, even if I felt young and inexperienced on the inside. Selling really is all about performance, whether you're selling someone a new tire or pitching a new product or even lobbying your boss for a promotion.

Today I look for those same performance-related qualities in the people I hire. I look for that confidence, that ability to talk, and that willingness to face fear. When I'm interviewing candidates for a job, I look for the skills in them that helped me succeed. Often I'll pick up some random object in my office—it could be a pen or a stapler or a watch—and ask them to sell it to me. It doesn't matter whether they know the product or are saying everything perfectly. What matters is how they perform, what story they tell about the object, and whether they focus on the right things.

Some people will take the pen and say, "Well, if you need a pen, this is one of them. It's got ink. It writes." That doesn't impress me. I'm looking for someone who keeps the focus on me as the potential buyer. He can say anything he wants about the object as long as it's about me and why *I* need the pen. If someone says, *"This pen feels so good in the hand, it just glides over the paper.*

It's a sophisticated pen for a sophisticated person," he's got me. As long as applicants listen and react to what I say, I know they know the basics of selling.

You can tell immediately if a person is a salesperson. Most people don't know what to do when you throw an impromptu sales test at them. They'll complain, "You caught me off guard!" That shows me they're coming from a place of fear and unpreparedness. One aspect of being a good businessman or businesswoman is being able to control the fear at any time.

A salesperson can never be caught off guard. When you walk in to sell something to somebody, you've got to be ready for the unexpected. Sure, as an inexperienced salesperson you never know what to expect, but don't just blurt out the first nonsense that comes into your head. Don't show your fear. Think quickly. Listen. Talk. Look that person in the eye and make her believe in you. Tailor your pitch to the person in front of you. She'll tell you what she wants if you listen closely enough. Is she after status or quality or instant gratification? If she criticizes your merchandise, what terms does she use? Does she say, "I'm really looking for something more upmarket"? Or "Our customers need to save money"? Or "We only carry top-quality items"? These kinds of comments will tell you what's important to her. Listening closely will tell you how to shape your selling pitch.

As a salesperson you're a performer. And plenty of world-class performers get stage fright. Famous opera singers, athletes, musicians, politicians—they all struggle with stage fright. Stage fright is universal in that a person's job or level of education doesn't matter; anyone can have it. The only thing that makes a difference is how you handle that fear so you're confident about doing the task in front of you. Experience does help in one sense because once you've made a sale a thousand times, you can be more confident that you'll do it again. But that doesn't mean you won't still be afraid. It just means you'll get better at dealing with fear.

I still deal with fear every day, but I've learned how not to show it. I certainly felt the butterflies when we first started filming *Hardcore Pawn*. But I couldn't show it because everyone had to see Les Gold, pawnbroker, on the screen, not someone shaking with fear!

It's not easy. It's taken me years to learn how to manage my fear. But you've got to learn to look people in the eye and project confidence even though you're afraid—afraid of failing, afraid of losing an opportunity, afraid of proving all those people right who said you'd never amount to anything. That fear isn't going to go away. But if you face it and perform in spite of your fear, you can learn to control it. Think of Indiana Jones. He hated snakes—was absolutely terrified of them—but that didn't stop him from walking through that pit. You've got to be like Indy and face your fears head-on.

When the Fear Is Armed and Dangerous

My fear of becoming the failure my father said I was was not a healthy fear. It was a trauma I've had to overcome, but in the end, it was a fear I was able to manage. The nerves you get when you're trying to make a sale or are about to walk into a big meeting are natural and understandable—and they're manageable for most of us.

But sometimes fear—a deep, visceral reaction—is absolutely necessary because what you're afraid of is imminent danger. In the case of physical threats, fear can actually keep you safe. As a pawnbroker working in a tough area in Detroit, I know this better than anyone.

In 1971, when I was twenty-one, I was working in the shop on New Year's Eve. I was one of three employees on the floor. L.G. was upstairs in the little office. It was around noon, and there were twenty-five customers in the store—New Year's Eve was a busy day for us back then. The day was going smoothly, even well, with customers eager to get quick cash to celebrate the holiday or to pay off some Christmas bills.

Suddenly, three people with guns burst in the front door.

"Put your hands up!" they shouted. I instantly put my hands up.

Then they yelled, "Put your hands down!" I put my hands back down. I couldn't tell whether they were more scared of me or I was more scared of them. But they had the guns. And they were after our cash and jewelry.

They told me to go into our back room and get down on the floor. They herded all the customers and an employee in with me—twenty-seven people in a tiny room.

I had a dog named Adam back then—not a guard dog or anything, just a pet, but I used to bring him to work with me. I said, "Please, don't hurt my dog." I couldn't focus on myself at that moment. I wasn't sure whether I was going to live through the next few minutes. But right then I was more worried about the dog than I was about my own life.

One of the thugs with guns said, "Don't worry, I won't. I like dogs."

At this point, my dad came downstairs from the office to see what the yelling was about, and he walked right into the scene—customers and me all down on the ground in the back room, people lying half on top of one another, all of us terrified.

Instantly a gun was pointed at him. "You got the keys to the safe?" one of the gunmen asked.

L.G. said he did, and walked over to the wall safe at the back of the store. While opening the safe, he hit the holdup alarm. It was a silent alarm, so nobody knew he'd done it—including me. As far as I knew, nobody was coming to help us.

A few minutes went by. It felt like hours.

All of a sudden I heard gunshots from outside the front of the store. I didn't know what was happening. But my dad did. He knew he'd hit the alarm, so he knew the cops had arrived. I found out later that the cops had shot the lookout guy out front.

The crooks heard the shots and ran out to the front of the store in a panic. L.G. immediately jumped up and ran downstairs, to hide out in the basement. He jammed a fifty-horsepower outboard motor against the door so no one could get in: not the gunmen, not the customers. Not even me, his son. He left me outside the door with twenty-five customers and one employee.

I shouted to everybody, "Stay where you are!" I ran to the storage room and got a shotgun, moving fast before the crooks came back and saw what I was doing.

As I ran back to the room where everybody was waiting, I saw a dead cop on the floor of the store. He had been the first one in through the door, and one of the robbers had shot him. His brains were splattered on the floor. I was twenty-one years old when this incident happened, and that image is still with me.

I ran past the body and kept running straight into the back room, where all those terrified people were still waiting, stunned. And then I realized something. I had the drop on the bad guys.

I ran back into the showroom. One of them, the one who'd promised not to kill my dog, was down on the floor near the front of the store, bleeding from his stomach, unconscious. A second guy begged me not to kill him. With my dad still downstairs, I realized it was up to me to take care of the situation. I had never seen a dead body before. I had never dealt with anything like this, but I didn't have a choice. There was nobody there to deal with it except me. So I just pointed the gun at the second guy and waited.

The front door burst open, and I found myself staring at the cops—the rest of the team, with guns drawn. I was holding a shotgun in my hand with a dead cop on the ground in front of me. I can't imagine how bad that must have looked. I quickly yelled, "Hey, guys, I'm on your team!"

They yelled back, "Les, it's OK, we know who you are."

That experience changed me. I realized I was going to live with some sense of fear every day I worked at the pawnshop—and even if it got as bad as that situation did, I could overcome it and keep going. And that was not the only time our store got held up. Far from it. Two years in a row, 1979 and 1980, we were robbed on December 5. The first time, the security guard went for the robber and got shot in the hip. The thief got away with about $80,000 worth of jewelry. When the next robbery happened, the same night one year later, I couldn't believe it! That crook got scared and left, so nobody got hurt. My wife's sister used to work for me at that time, but after the second robbery, she'd never work on that day again.

The time we were robbed in 1984, I got hurt—but not by the crook. I was rushing into the store to find out what was going on and I ran right into the front door and broke my nose.

My father was seriously injured during another robbery. A crook came into Sam's Loan disguised as a woman, and he and his associates managed to take my dad downstairs, where they beat him up pretty badly. They broke both his eye sockets. As they were leaving, they got into a shootout with the cops. My dad got shot. One of the holdup men was killed.

After that, my dad closed up the store. He basically stopped doing business because he was scared to go to work. That may be understandable, but it's also unacceptable. As scary as it is, terrible things do happen in life. People get hit by the proverbial bus even when they're in safe lines of work. Businesses get robbed—banks, jewelry stores, liquor stores, and pawnshops. You can't be a pawnbroker and be afraid to go to work. My father practically put Sam's Loan out of business because he couldn't face that fear. In the end, my father's fear did put him out of business.

Although most businesses don't put you in situations where you're in fear for your life, you do face other real threats. If you're the only person providing for your family, worrying about them is a fear—a healthy one, one that keeps you hungry and productive. If your company is going through a round of layoffs, that's a real threat. If you're starting a new business, it makes sense to be worried about making payroll and keeping the lights on. It's important to remember that anytime you face a real threat from outside yourself, you can't control what anyone else is going to do, but you can control how you respond.

When I was in that holdup, I couldn't control what my dad or the robbers or the cops were going to do. I didn't have all the information that my dad did, and I didn't know what the situation looked like from anyone else's perspective. That kind of uncertainty is terrifying, and it should be terrifying. You have to accept these big fears and respond to the situation in the best way you can.

Afraid Every Day

When I was twenty-eight we opened a second store, and when I was thirty-one I ended my financial partnership with my father and focused entirely on that second store as my solo venture. When I split with my father and took over the new store, we made about five to seven loans a day. I was constantly afraid I'd run out of cash and wouldn't be able to keep making loans. I had empty showcases sometimes.

My business struggled for a long time. I struggled to pay my bills. I got into the red pretty badly. At one point I owed the electric company $30,000 and the IRS $50,000. I'd shuffle things around, rob Peter to pay Paul, pay a little bit here and a little bit there because I needed to put as much money as I possibly could back into the business. I strung things along like that for as long as I could, afraid every day, until eventually I got on a payment plan with everybody.

I remember once during this time when my wife and I took the kids to the state fair. They wanted some money to go on the rides, but Lili and I only had twenty dollars. We made sure the kids went on the rides, and we bought them dinner, too. Lili and I skipped dinner that night. We didn't have the cash, but we never wanted the kids to know we were in trouble.

Lili was a real source of strength for me during this time. I had a vision of what my business could be, but when I'd come home at the end of the day worried about whether we'd make it through the next day, she would assure me that we'd make it. Every day. You know how they say that behind every successful man is a strong woman? Well, in my case that's really true. I faced endless fears every day when American Jewelry and Loan was getting started, but I was lucky enough to face those fears with somebody at my side giving me the emotional strength to keep going.

Knowing that I was working for my family made me stronger, too. I did whatever I possibly could to raise money. When money was tight, nothing I owned was sacred to me. If you wanted my shirt, I'd sell it to you. I even sold some of my own jewelry from time to time. The fear of not being able to grow my business was driving me on, and nothing was off-limits.

I lived with the fear of not making money for ten years. Every day I was afraid to open the doors of my shop. Even though I loved selling and I was good at it, even though I had grown up in a pawnshop, I was overcome with fear. Somehow I'd get through the day, even though all day I was afraid I wouldn't make it to closing. I'd close up, go home, and then I'd get up the next morning and do it again. I was afraid I might have to say no to somebody who wanted a loan—and if you start saying no to your customers, you can't grow. But most of all, I was afraid of failing altogether, and proving my dad right.

Making Fear Work for You

Being afraid of failing can be a crippling fear. If you're always worrying about making a mistake, you're going to end up frozen in place. You won't want to do anything at all because you're afraid it might be the wrong thing. But that fear can also push you to work harder, to try something new, to take a risk that might help you to grow. For me, the fear my father instilled in me was a fear of not succeeding. It was a fear of proving him right, showing him that I was a loser. That's what keeps pushing me to think bigger and work harder.

If you find that your fear is keeping you stuck in place, it's time to think about it in a different way. Are you afraid of walking into your boss's office and asking for a promotion? Try telling yourself you're not so much afraid of the conversation going badly as you are afraid of being stuck in this stage in your career. You'll definitely stay stuck if you don't have this important conversation. Your fear can help push you forward.

Fortunately, my business is strong enough now that I don't have to worry that I won't be able to make loans. But I'm still afraid of losing a chance to grow. A year ago one of my competitors went out of business. His shop had been open for ninety years, but it hadn't been making loans for almost a year. The owner came to me and asked if I wanted to buy out his inventory—all the merchandise he had in pawn that people were still making payments on. He told me he had $5 million in outstanding loans. Every single item in that inventory represented an income stream from the interest. I could have been buying an extra $1.5 million a year.

I thought to myself, *If I can put this deal together, I can't lose*. But I didn't have $5 million to give my competitor. I was so scared I was going to lose the deal to someone else, I was losing sleep over it. But when I sent my people to go through his inventory, it turned out that it wasn't nearly as valuable as he'd thought. He had never used a computer, and over time the numbers got away from him. His totals were simply wrong: too high by a considerable amount. With the right numbers, I had the cash to buy him out, and we made the deal. Not only did I get that income stream, but his loyal customers became my customers. In that case, my fear of losing pushed me to a big win.

Over the years I've created the persona of the ultimate salesman. I don't let my fear show when I'm on the shop floor. But the fear my father instilled in me has stayed with me for years. I had to keep proving him wrong again and again. The facade I had on the outside, the part that people saw, was that of a believer. But that successful persona was always in conflict with the part of me that didn't believe. I faced that fear every day.

I know I will never outgrow the fear of losing out to somebody bigger or quicker or just luckier than me. Part of me hopes I never do. Although I ultimately made that deal to buy out the other pawnshop, I know I could have lost it. I can still fail; that's part of what keeps me striving.

Failure can push you forward. Michael Jordan said this in a famous Nike commercial: "I've missed more than nine thousand shots in my career. I've lost almost three hundred games. Twenty-six times I've been trusted to take the game-winning shot and missed. I've failed over and over and over again in my life. And that is why I succeed."

I'm no Michael Jordan, but I am successful. And I know he's right: You can't avoid failure. You have to push past it. You have to face your fear and make it work for you. Take the fears that are holding you back and turn them around so they become fears that motivate you. Tell yourself you're not afraid of failing; you're afraid of not succeeding. You're not afraid of being fired; you're afraid of not being promoted. Face your fear and find a way to let it push you forward instead of holding you back.

[CHAPTER 2]

Believe in Yourself

I know I'm not the only person in the world who had a tough childhood or has struggled with self-doubt. The question is, how do we get past that doubt? How do we learn to believe in ourselves? In this chapter I'll show you how to build your confidence, step-by-step, until you're as big and as bad as I am. You'll learn

+ **to find a supportive voice;**
+ **to set yourself up to win small victories;**
+ **to *expect* to fail;**
+ **to learn from failure; and**
+ **to commit to making the long journey to success.**

My Biggest Fan

In order to be successful you have to learn to believe in yourself with at least half your heart. When you hear a voice—for me it's my father's voice—that says you're never going to amount to anything, you've got to find a voice that argues back. You may never escape that negative, belittling voice, but you've got to have an equally strong voice that takes your side.

While I was growing up, my Popsie was my positive voice and my biggest supporter. By the time I was born, he was running a small but successful pawnshop called Sam's Loan, at Michigan Avenue and Fifth Street in Detroit. That's the store I grew up in, the place where I learned to be a salesman. That was my business school. I still have the old sign in my office: "Sam's Loan—Money in 1 Minute."

When I was a kid, Popsie was my hero. By the time I came along, America wasn't the same place he'd come to when he was a teenager. I remember the first time he went on an airplane—he told me that he couldn't quite believe the plane had moved. I guess it was a little different from that horse and buggy. But he was a smart man and a sharp businessman, and he'd do anything for his family. He taught me to work hard, get a good day's pay, and always put family first. Growing up with the father I had, I always admired how successful Popsie was, and how dedicated he was to his kids and grandkids.

My parents lived with my grandparents for the first two and a half years of my life, but even when we moved out, we didn't go very far. For most of my childhood we lived three blocks away from Popsie and Bubbie. To escape my parents' fighting and my dad's constant put-downs, after school I'd walk to their house. It was my safe zone. Popsie would let me sleep in his bed, and I'd feel safer surrounded by the smell of the pipe he always smoked.

I'd spend the whole weekend with my grandparents whenever I could. On Fridays, I'd sleep over at my grandparents' house, and then almost every Saturday morning my grandfather would take me to work with him at Sam's Loan. I had all week to hang out with my friends—on Saturdays, I wanted to be with Popsie, talking to him and learning from him. We'd go out to breakfast and then go to Katz's Deli and buy hot dogs for lunch and spend the day in the store. It meant a lot to me to think I was learning a trade, like I was going to be able to support myself when the time came.

Nobody could really protect me from my father. Even Popsie, as supportive as he was, was physically intimidated by him. Popsie was a lot smarter than my father, but he wasn't a big guy. Yet he knew what it was like for me in that house and he would always listen if I wanted to talk. I felt like I could count on him for unbiased advice. I knew he wouldn't think about anything other than what was going to be best for me.

I spent as much time as I could with Popsie. The family used to go on vacations without my father sometimes, because somebody had to stay and run the store. And to be honest, I'm sure my father felt more comfortable letting us go without him. He knew what Popsie and Bubbie thought of him. So the rest of us would visit my aunt in New Jersey. My cousins were a few years older than me, so they didn't always want me hanging around them. But I was closer to Popsie than they were, so I still enjoyed those vacations. Popsie and I used to play a game we called Nuts. We'd take filbert nuts and roll them down a piece of wood, trying to hit the other nuts that were scattered on the floor. If you hit one, you'd scoop up all the nuts on the floor, and whoever ended up with the most nuts was the winner.

Being around Popsie helped me a lot. He loved me. He didn't make me feel bad about myself, and I could always rely on him. If I had a problem, he was the one I wanted to talk to. I'd go to him with school troubles, anything that came up. He might not totally understand what I was talking about—the world in the 1950s was a lot different from what it was when he was young—but he would always listen, and I'd feel better knowing he was on my side. He was standing right there, encouraging me, when I made my very first sale at seven years old.

Back in grade school I wasn't known as a tough guy. I was kind of a shy kid, and I wasn't very good at academics. There were a lot of reasons for me to believe that my dad was right and I was never going to be successful. But Popsie was always there for me. Whatever I needed, he'd help me out. I saw him make so many sacrifices for his family, like when my uncle's business was on the rocks and he stepped in to make sure my aunt and my cousins would still have a roof over their heads. He was generous and always wanted me to be happy. When I was twelve I started saving up to buy my first car. My dream ride was a 1965 Mustang, green with a white vinyl top. This was the car of a lifetime for me. Popsie told me, "If you save five hundred dollars by the time you're sixteen, I'll match it." Just the fact that he said that made me think he believed I could do it.

Popsie died of a heart attack in 1969, when I was eighteen. My mother and grandmother and I were together in the hospital when the doctors told us he had passed. It was a terrifying day for me because while I was growing up, he was it—he was the one who believed in me. I think I felt the way a lot of people feel when their parents die: like I'd lost a protector, like I suddenly had to step up and be a man, and I wasn't really ready for it.

When it came time to divide up his possessions, there were two things I wanted. I didn't care about getting any money. I just wanted something that would always remind me of him. So I took the hat he wore every week to synagogue—a brown hat with a feather on the side—and I took his pipe. Looking at those two things made me feel like he was still close to me. I could look at those mementos and remember his voice and how safe I'd felt surrounded by the smell of that pipe. I'd remember the days we spent at the pawnshop and the lessons he taught me about how to deal with customers, how to be successful, how to be a good man.

Life is all about learning to live with loss, and I miss Popsie every day. What I've learned is that you don't get to keep people forever, but you do get to keep memories of them. I can still hear Popsie calling me "boychik." I have his voice in my mind, and I will never forget the lessons he taught me.

Today my grandkids call me Popsie, and that means the world to me. I broke down and cried when Ashley asked me if her kids could call me that. And now it's even spread beyond our family; my grandkids' friends call me Popsie, too. I hope I can be even half as supportive of this new generation as Popsie was of me. If I emulate my grandfather in any way, I'll know I've done something right in my life.

Find a Supportive Voice

I believe everyone needs an advocate like Popsie. Believing in yourself isn't easy. Your doubts and your fears will always be with you. So you need to look for someone in your life who can become your cheering section. Maybe he or she is a spouse, a friend, a teacher, a family friend.

Whenever you hear that voice in your head that says you're never going to amount to anything, stop for a moment and remember your cheerleader. Remember your Popsie. Try to think of a specific time he said something encouraging or supportive. Try to picture his face. Hear his voice in your head. Then ask yourself, who am I going to prove right, the person who tells me I'm nothing or the person who knows that I'm somebody? That's a choice you make every day, so choose positively.

It is essential to answer your doubts every time they come up. If you let them linger, thinking that you'll deal with them later when you're feeling stronger or when your life improves, those doubts will continue to drag you down every minute you fail to deal with them. You have to replace the negativity with positive thoughts and voices. Let's say you're a manager and your team isn't achieving its goals. You start to think you're just bad at your job. As soon as that thought pops into your head, stop. Tell yourself that there are probably ways you can improve, but that doesn't mean you're a failure. It just means you need to keep working at the task. Tell yourself everyone has those feelings sometimes—but you get to choose how to respond to them. Remember your supportive voice and resolve to keep trying.

If you don't think you have anybody who is really supporting you, consider asking for help. Believe me, I know how hard that can be. When I lost Popsie and felt like I had to step into his shoes, I didn't think there was ever going to be anybody else I could lean on the way I had leaned on him. But I know now that to reach big goals, you've got to believe you can reach them, and to do that, you're going to need a supportive voice in your life. These days I have my wife supporting me, and I'm blessed to have her. I couldn't have built American Jewelry and Loan without her, and you're not going to achieve your goals without somebody on your side. If you're building a business, consider reaching out to another businessperson in your community. Join the chamber of commerce or an industry organization. Talk to people at your synagogue or church or mosque. Take a class or go to some networking events and find someone who's got a similar goal so you can support each other.

Finding someone to support you is the first step in a long journey. You're going to have to work hard to learn to believe in yourself. But you won't be able to do it alone. You need to find a supportive voice.

Start with Small Victories

Finding a supporter or two will make a huge difference, but it's only the first step. You also have to start proving to yourself that your supporters are right about you. My mother and I had a better relationship than my father and I did. She loved and supported me. She believed in me. When I was about twelve years old, I made her a table in shop class, a little square side table with ceramic tiles set in the top. She said it was so beautiful, she thought I could sell it. Most kids would be unhappy if they gave Mom a gift and she said, "Let's sell this." But growing up in a family of salespeople, that was the biggest compliment someone could give me.

My mom went with me to the hardware store and we bought the materials to make more side tables. I must have sold about a hundred of them, at twenty dollars a pair. At first I sold them to my mom's friends, and then after a while my cousin showed them to a friend who worked at a small department store, and they started selling them there.

I loved making a profit. It empowered me. My mom's support of my early work helped me believe I was sharp, that I wasn't going to be the failure that my father said I was. Scoring those little victories of selling my tables was proof that I could be somebody. It was the next step toward disproving my dad and proving to myself that I was talented. I still have one of those tables in my house.

Every deal I made, every table I sold, was a tangible accomplishment, and it was a way to see myself as a provider helping to support my family the way Popsie always did. I'm not the only one who believes small victories are important: Psychologists say that the key to changing your life is to set small, achievable goals so that you experience a lot of little victories along the way to meeting your larger goal.

It's not going to be enough just to tell yourself you can succeed, or listen to somebody in your life who believes in you. That kind of support is a place to start, but you're also going to need some real accomplishments to build your confidence. For me, Popsie's pawnshop was the perfect ground on which to build those small victories.

In a pawnshop, buying and selling are stripped down to their essentials. You're not selling cars or perfume or any single constant thing—you're selling whatever's on the floor that day. You're not buying based on a budget or what you think you're going to need next week or what you think is going to be fashionable in six months. You're buying anything and everything that walks into the store, at the best price you can get.

I never know what's going to come in the door on any given day, and I need to be ready for anything. That's the fun, and the fear, of a business that's constantly changing. It keeps you growing, and flexible, and it keeps you sharp. Most of all, it forces you to focus on the basics.

When you look at the bones of buying and selling, you can see that it's all about belief. You've got to believe in yourself in order to project the confidence you need to win over your customer. You've got to believe in the product and in your own ability to figure out what it's worth. And you've got to believe in your ability to negotiate and represent your own interest without turning off the customer. You never truly know that you're going to make the deal. A million things can happen during a negotiation. As a salesperson, you might focus on a feature the customer doesn't care about, or say something that reminds her of a big purchase she just made. Another employee or customer in the store might interject and disrupt the rapport you were building. For those reasons and more, I'm still afraid of not making a sale—especially when the cameras are rolling for *Hardcore Pawn*! But you have to learn how to hide that fear and project confidence, so you can convince your customer—and yourself—that you believe you will succeed. And in order to learn to do that, you've got to set yourself up to win small victories along the way, so you can start to prove to yourself that you're worth believing in.

• • •

Expect to Fail

You won't win every time. Working in pawnshops has taught me that you have to expect to hear the word "No." You're going to hear it a lot. You're going to fail, and you're going to keep failing.

I still make mistakes, big ones occasionally. We recently had a customer come into the shop with an Audemars Piguet, a luxury Swiss watch from the Royal Oak collection, which would typically retail for something like $15,000. I opened up the box and checked out the watch, with Seth, my jeweler Jeff, and Ashley all looking on. This was a beautiful watch. The Royal Oak collection stands out because of its simplicity—it was the first luxury watch to use stainless steel, so the value is in the name and the design, including the eight hexagonal screws that surround the face.

I've been in this business long enough to feel pretty confident that I know how to spot a fake watch. I took the watch apart and checked it out. It looked perfect, so I bought it for $5,000, maybe a third of what you'd pay retail for a real Royal Oak. I actually thought about keeping this watch—it was so beautiful—but I wanted to make some money, so I turned around and sold it for $9,000.

The next day the person I sold the watch to came back into the store and demanded his money back. He said the watch was a fake. He had taken it to an expert and it turned out to be an almost perfect replica—almost—but the screws were just a millimeter too short to be a real Audemars Piguet. I had to refund his money and I lost thousands of dollars on that deal.

Of course, it's not just deals I make mistakes on. I'm happy to say that most of my business decisions are good ones, but I do sometimes make business mistakes.

I was quick to jump into selling electronics when personal computers started taking off, but I didn't quite realize how quickly the technology would keep changing. Usually a pawnshop is a great home for old stuff. There's always somebody out there willing to buy something old if it's cheap enough. I kept selling black-and-white TVs for years after color TVs came out. I even used to sell a screen you could put over a black-and-white TV to make it look like it was in color. So when my customers started bringing in computers, I'd buy them or make loans on them the same as I would for a TV or another piece of equipment. My theory always was that if somebody bought it once, somebody else would want it again. And if you wait long enough, old junk turns into antiques, right?

But PC technology changed a lot faster than what I was used to. I've had to throw some computers right into the Dumpster because they were just not worth enough money anymore to keep them around. I'm still learning to keep up. Just recently I pulled five hundred laptops out of pawn, computers that people weren't able to redeem—or maybe they'd just decided not to bother because the technology was worth 60 percent less now than it was a year and a half ago. So we're lowering the price we're selling them for. We need to sell them quick or they're headed for the Dumpster, too.

No matter how long I walk that pawnshop floor, I know I'm going to keep making mistakes. But the great thing about a pawnshop is there's always another deal coming in the door. If you don't make this deal, you'll make the next one. When you fail, you can take a few minutes to think about what went wrong and how you're going to do things differently next time—and then you move on. Somebody else is walking in the door, and you've got another chance to prove yourself. As long as you can make the next deal better than the last one, you're going to be successful.

No matter where you work, you have to expect to fail. We all fail sometimes. Think of it this way: You can't succeed without failing. Your boss didn't get to where he is by never making a mistake. That woman in the C-suite with the beautiful panoramic view from her office—she's made a lot of mistakes on her way up there. Expect it, deal with it, learn to fix it.

. . .

Learn from Your Failures

I tell Seth and Ashley that I'm depending on them to make mistakes. I tell my employees that, too. You need those mistakes in order to learn what to do when things go wrong.

One of my longest-serving employees, Brian, bought a fake Patek Philippe watch the other day when I was out of town. He paid $2,000 for it. Now, obviously, this is something that just happens sometimes. Happens to me, too, as you've seen. But in this case, when I got back to the shop, I took one look at the watch and I could tell that it was a fake. The writing on the face was all wrong, and when I opened it up, I saw immediately that the mechanical part of the watch didn't move right. Brian's still learning all the little tricks I know to spot a fake.

Brian's the type of guy who will really beat himself up over a mistake. He's like me in that when he was growing up, he was told he wasn't going to amount to anything. So I'm trying to be that supportive voice for him. When I told him the watch was fake, I also made sure to tell him that it was no big deal. If you make a legitimate mistake and you're up front about it with me, we don't have a problem. We can live with it. As long as I didn't lose my license, we didn't do anything illegal, and nobody got hurt, then this mistake is just an opportunity to learn. Next time, he'll know what to look for to spot that type of fake.

That's why failure is so important—it's the only way you're going to learn. Your successes just confirm your hunch that you're a genius, right? They don't do anything to help you grow. If you have a success, all you can do is repeat it. But failures teach you what you don't know, and they help you find out more about your marketplace and your business.

There's one other thing that failure does: It keeps you honest. It's easy to get a little full of yourself once you achieve a big goal. It's easy to start thinking that you always know what's best and you don't really need to listen to anybody else. But you are never too big to fail. Working in a pawnshop keeps me honest because I still fail to make deals. I still hear the word "No." The pawn business won't let me forget that every day, every deal, is a new opportunity. Every deal can be a "Yes."

We sell a lot of musical instruments in the store. Recently a customer came in with a Gibson Les Paul guitar. Don, our employee who usually takes care of guitars and actually knows something about them, wasn't there that day. But I've been a pawnbroker my whole life, and I figured I could handle it. After examining the guitar, I went to the back of the shop and quickly looked up Les Paul guitars online. After some quick online research, I thought the customer's guitar looked OK according to what I'd found, so I bought it for $900.

The next day Don came back and he could tell pretty quickly that the guitar was a fake. The wires on the inside of the guitar were the wrong color. I paid a hefty price for the reminder that no matter how many years I've been in this business, I don't know everything about everything. I can still be had.

If you're not lucky enough to work in a pawnshop, you're going to have to create similar kinds of conditions for yourself so you can practice hearing "No" and failing and making mistakes and pushing on anyway. You might start by practicing in a lower-stakes environment, like raising money for a charity you believe in, negotiating for a better deal on your cable bill, or helping out with a voter registration drive. When you get more comfortable with the idea of hearing "No," practice being ready to hear it about something that matters by asking for more than you think you can get in a negotiation, asking for a raise at work, or asking for a better deal from a supplier. That's what I did when I started selling those chains to little boutiques. I heard "No" a lot, but I just walked into the next shop and tried again. I kept trying until I made a sale and proved to myself that I could do it.

If you expect to fail, if you get used to hearing "No," you won't let it throw you. If you learn from failure, your mistakes will build your belief in yourself instead of undermining it. If you learn from failure, it'll make you more confident, not less.

Make a Commitment

Small victories will build your confidence and get you started on the road to success. But I've never been content to stop there, and I hope you're not, either. Those small victories should inspire you to seek out bigger challenges. To become truly successful, to realize your biggest dreams, you're going to need to change your life. Big goals require big sacrifices. But if you've built up a series of small victories, you will know that you're capable of winning. That knowledge will help you find the confidence to make a commitment to changing your life in pursuit of your dreams.

You're not going to learn to believe in yourself in an afternoon. If you struggle with self-doubt, believe me, I sympathize. I've been there. Yes, I had Popsie on my side. Yes, I learned to sell early in my life. Yes, I was able to start making money and proving myself when I was still young, but my journey hasn't been a straight upward climb. Back in 1980, when I first went out on my own with American Jewelry and Loan, it was difficult to maintain my belief that the store would succeed. I was struggling to keep enough cash on hand to keep making loans. I was also having a hard time believing in myself.

As a result, I had a real eating problem in the early 1990s. I used to buy a half gallon of mocha chip ice cream and add cake to it. I ate a tub of this ice cream–cake concoction every two days. I'd also have two Burger King milk shakes a day, and a pound of M&M's every other day. I piled on the weight until I ballooned to 236 pounds. I used to stand in front of the mirror and say to myself, "I hate you, you big, fat pig." I basically felt like I couldn't stand being Les Gold anymore. That was the lowest point in my life.

I decided to go on a diet, but I wasn't going to call it a diet because diets fail. They fail because you're kidding yourself that you're only going to have to make this effort for a little while. You tell yourself, *I just need to lose ten pounds, and then the diet's over.* So I didn't go on a diet—I made a lifestyle change.

And luckily, somebody stepped in to help me. My jeweler, Jeff, found me a trainer. He saw I wanted to make a change and he wanted to help me out. I started losing weight. I started to get my health and life back together. I made a commitment to change the way I ate and exercised.

The only way to truly change your life is to be honest with yourself and admit that that's what you're doing. You can't kid yourself that a lifestyle change is really just a little tweak and you'll hardly notice the difference. You have to accept that you'll never go back to your bad old habits and that although it's going to be hard, it's going to be worth the effort. You need to acknowledge that whatever change you make won't just be a temporary push. It's not like working hard to meet some deadline, and then being able to relax and watch TV every night when it's over. You need to commit to making a permanent lifestyle change. Call it what it is. Make a commitment to do whatever it takes to make this change.

You also have to learn to love the change you're making. Focus on what you're getting, the benefits, not the thing you're giving up. For example, I gave up a lot of foods I used to love, but I gained a new routine that helps me focus on my work. My morning workout has become a time when I reflect and prepare for the day ahead.

If you're happy with your life the way it is, then you don't need to change. Not everybody has to be a business owner or a millionaire. And I know you can be perfectly happy at any size and shape. Personally, maybe because I heard so much negativity when I was a kid, or maybe because I've just never been able to do anything in moderation, a little bit of success was never going to be enough. I want to win and I want to win big. So I focused on the goal I was shooting for—in this case, my weight loss—and I thought about how good I would feel when I got there, and I started proving I could do it, step-by-step.

I made a huge lifestyle change and I made it for keeps. I completely changed the way I eat: good-bye Burger King milk shakes, hello plain grilled chicken and steamed vegetables. My favorite food in the world used to be fried chicken. I haven't had a single piece in more than seventeen years. I eat pretty much the same thing every day of the week, year after year. You might think of that as deprivation, but for me it's liberating. I gave up M&M's, but I gained a new life, a new me, a new sense of self-respect. This was another chance for me to prove to myself that I could succeed in anything I put my mind to, and every morning when I get up and go to the gym, every evening when I eat another plate of grilled chicken, I'm proving it to myself all over again.

I still set big goals for myself. That's how I approached doing *Hardcore Pawn,* our TV show, as well. If I was going to spend hundreds of hours making a TV show, I wanted it to be a hit. I set a big goal for the show: to reach 3 million viewers. The folks at the network told me it would never happen because the channel wasn't big enough; truTV just didn't get those kinds of ratings. Well, I set out to prove that we could do it anyway. I worked hard on that show. I went out of my way to do as many promotional events as I possibly could. I appeared on *Good Morning America* and the Fox Business channel, talking up the show. I said yes to every possible opportunity to make the show more successful. And we did it. We hit 3 million viewers. Now I'm moving that bar even higher. Next up: 3.5 million. I also set a goal of completing one hundred shows. Recently we finished number 107. There's no stopping us now.

Doing this show has required another lifestyle change. Once we made the decision to go on TV, there was no turning back. Everywhere I go now, people come up to me to say they watch the show and to shake my hand and get their picture taken with me. But like I said before, the key to making a lifestyle change is to love the new version of your life. I'm not going to be one of those celebrities who complains about losing his privacy. Sure, some days I just want a quiet meal with my family when I'm out and about, but as long as people are reasonable about it, I love talking to fans. It's a daily reminder that I'm succeeding in this goal I've set myself. I get a kick out of meeting all the different kinds of people who watch the show.

I always remember that I'm a pawnbroker who just happens to be a TV personality—not a TV personality who happens to be a pawnbroker. The show will not last forever, but I will always be a pawnbroker.

If you're aiming for a big, ambitious goal, like building your own business or transforming your career, it's going to take a long time to achieve. Changing your life takes time. Be prepared for that. It took me years to lose the weight I wanted to lose. And it took me years to get to the point where I had enough cash on hand to no longer worry about paying my bills and being able to keep making loans. The same qualities got me to both goals: determination, confidence, belief in myself, and a willingness to make sacrifices in the service of a really big, life-changing goal.

If you're an entrepreneur, you're not going to build a multimillion-dollar business overnight. Building a business the way I did, starting from scratch with the $20,000 I'd saved up, takes an incredible amount of time and dedication. But it is possible to build a business with basically nothing. I've done it and, of course, I'm not the only one. It's not easy, but it can be done. You need to remember, though, to stay committed to your big goals and not get discouraged when you don't have results overnight.

Aim toward any goal one step, one day at a time. Deal with today's challenges today because tomorrow there'll be something else. But you're never going to be big unless you make little strides every day. And you'll never reach your goal unless you're honest with yourself about how long it's going to take and how big a change it's going to require you to make. Learning to believe in yourself as you aim for success is not a temporary push; it's a lifestyle change. You've got to commit to making the long journey to success.

[CHAPTER 3]

Love What You Do

In thirty-six years, my wife, Lili, has never once woken up in the morning and heard me say, "I don't want to go to work today." Going to work for me is like going on a first date every single day; my heart actually starts to beat faster when I get near the store. I'm blessed to work in a uniquely entertaining business, but I believe anyone can find joy in work if he or she is willing to, well, work for it. In this chapter, I'll show you how you can learn to love your work if you're willing to

+ **embrace change;**
+ **focus on connecting with people; and**
+ **commit to making the effort.**

Endless Variety

I love what I do. Honestly, I think anybody would. Pawnbroking is a business like no other. In a lifetime of pawnbroking, I've sold everything from shoes to stripper poles, from cappuccino machines to mounted bobcats. That's what makes this work so exciting—I never know what's going to happen when I walk in that door.

We get everything in our store. We had James Jamerson's grandkids come in and sell us a bass that was made for him. That's a piece of Detroit history—a bass made for a hometown guy who played on more than thirty-one hits for Motown Records. I've bought movie props—a customer once brought in a zombie made for a movie. He'd paid $2,500 for it, and he was asking for $1,500. I said I'd flip a coin and give him either $300 or $100. I got it for $100.

And yes, I've bought and sold some more *interesting* stuff, too. The stripper pole made it onto our show, but you probably didn't see the sex-swing stand. Or the woman who brought in a cart full of sex toys. Or the woman who brought in a gynecological exam table that she'd been using to do piercings on. Each of those items was a completely new experience for me. I'd never bought or sold any of those things before they were brought into my store. But my philosophy is that if somebody bought it once, somebody else is going to want it again. If we put it out on the floor, it'll sell.

Just about everything finds a buyer. Even that gynecological table sold, and on the very same day I bought it. A customer walked in and said, "What's that?"

I explained what it was.

He said, "Can you have sex on it?"

Hey, he bought it—my philosophy also is that he can do whatever he wants with it.

Though some of my purchases may seem out there, even I won't buy absolutely everything. Some guy came in recently with a thousand hissing cockroaches. He wanted a hundred dollars for them. Those I did not buy. We have enough creatures in the store without buying more.

Sometimes when people get really desperate, they'll try to sell themselves, essentially. There's a plasma donation center down the street from us, and there are days when you can't even get a parking spot because there are so many people lining up to sell their blood. When times are desperate, people will do desperate things. I've had people offer to sell me their kidneys. One guy tried to sell me two doses of HIV medication for $5,000. A woman came in and asked if she could pawn her children. I'm afraid she wasn't joking.

Obviously, I would never buy anything illegal or immoral. But I will take a chance on unusual things, such as a live alligator I took in pawn. We kept that in the store and fed it goldfish. The alligator is no longer with us, but the surviving goldfish are about a foot long now.

A woman came into the store recently with a high school locker. In that locker was a skeleton. She had paid $24 for a room full of stuff, *Storage Wars*–style, and she had no idea what was in it. We ended up paying her $400 for the skeleton. Those are worth a lot of money to medical schools; they can go for about $1,200.

I learned that (almost) anything goes when I worked in my grandfather's store while I was growing up. We used to sell suits, pants, hats, shoes. Of course, the usual pawnshop items are jewelry and electronics today. People sometimes brought in their cats and dogs. On one memorable occasion, when I was a kid, my father took a monkey in pawn. I came home from school and my father said, "Let's play a game called monkey in the closet!" I guess the joke was how freaked out I was to find out there really was a monkey in the closet. The customer was supposed to leave the monkey for only a day, but the monkey ended up living with us for a month. Thank goodness he finally did pick it up, because my mother was not at all pleased about having that animal in her house. Fortunately, monkeys are not a hot item in the pawnbroking world these days.

My goal for the TV show is to capture the endless sense of excitement I have for the variety of people, and their merchandise, who come in the front door of the store. My only rule is that I never want the producers to tell me anything about the customer I'm going to talk to ahead of time. When the cameras aren't there, if one of the employees on the floor gets a tough or unusual customer, he or she will get me to help out, filling me in on what's happened so far. But for *Hardcore Pawn,* I don't want to know anything before I walk up to that customer. I want to be genuinely surprised, and I want the viewer to see my reaction.

I think that's one reason the show is so successful. We're showing the viewer something that gets at the core of why I love my business—the constant change and surprises—and I think that excitement comes through. When you watch me on the show, you're seeing me deal with the crazy, unexpected, always-changing nature of the pawn business. And I think that excitement about the unknown is contagious.

Change Is the Only Constant

What's forever fun about the pawn business is that it's constantly changing. When I was a kid, at my grandfather's pawnshop, we sold guitars, guns, suitcases, television sets, and, of course, jewelry. But you have to change with the times. What was popular five years ago isn't popular today. Of course some items are held in pawn for years; we have to balance those items we hold in inventory against those we can sell. I love seeing the shop change as the customers bring in different kinds of things.

We never used to have much silver jewelry around in the shop, but about six years ago, one of my managers, Brian, told me that people were coming in and asking for silver. Now, I believe in listening to my customers. I'm not running a department store, and I don't have a whole buying department keeping an eye on trends, so my managers and I have to listen carefully to make sure we're selling what our customers want to buy. Today about a third of our jewelry cases are filled with silver.

That's part of a bigger change in precious metals. The price of gold has risen so much in the past ten years or so that people are looking for alternatives. Three years ago you couldn't sell tungsten jewelry, for example. There was no demand for it. But now gold and platinum and other metals have gotten so expensive, we sell jewelry made out of tungsten, resin, carbon fiber—every imaginable substitute for those expensive metals. That's just one example of the way the marketplace shifts with a changing economy, different tastes, and supply and demand. You've got to find ways to stay abreast of the changes in your business—and love that aspect of your workday—because it's what will keep you thriving.

Of course, all businesses change over time, not just pawnshops. Say you're a car dealer. You may be selling Ford pickup trucks year after year, but those pickup trucks change a little bit every year. There's always something new to learn about your product or your industry. Technology will change. What your customer wants will change. You have to learn to get excited about that stuff. Take the electronics world. It used to be all about the PC; now it's about tablets and smartphones. If you stay fixated on the PC, your customers will leave you way behind. You have to learn to embrace change (and love it), stay current, and keep your inventory appealing.

It's essential to your business success that you listen to your customers, survey the changes in the marketplace, and anticipate what people will want next. If you relax and stop caring about what's going on in your industry, the changes will pass you by, you'll become irrelevant, and you'll be out of business. That's the simple fact of the free market.

Sometimes change will be forced on you. Regulation will change or a recession will hit, and you'll have to adapt. Any business can face that kind of change, and you'll have to move quickly to keep your business running at full speed. You might have to change your products. You might have to change your back end, the support systems and technology you use. You might have to change your marketing or your pricing. Whatever the issue, you have to be prepared to shift when the market calls for it. Particularly in the current economy, you've got to be ready to change anything and everything about your business quickly to stay relevant. If you wait too long, your business will fail. Simple as that. You've got to keep growing. And that means you've got to keep changing.

You can't just sit back and wait for change to come. I push for change. For example, I started collecting and selling antiques before my customers started requesting them. I've always loved going to antique shops and flea markets. I happen to love old drugstore signs, old machinery, anything like that. So after the TV show started drawing in more middle-class customers, I was able to start selling antiques. As our customer changes, I want to keep changing our merchandise. We also sell new furniture now and have become a furniture distributor—another change I pushed for. It fills the center of the showroom floor in a nice way, and helps create the sense that, as a store, we've got more to offer than the classic pawnshop standbys like jewelry, fur coats, and televisions.

A few years ago I took over a second store in Pontiac, about twenty-five miles away, which I renamed American Jewelry and Loan—Pontiac. I love seeing how different that store is from our 8 Mile Road location. It's a different city and a different customer. The folks in Pontiac don't walk in and tell you how much they're hoping to get for their item. Instead, they say, "How much can you give me for it?" They make the salesman throw out the first price. And in a negotiation, throwing out the first price puts you at a bit of a disadvantage because you're showing your hand. So in Pontiac, the salesman has to be a little savvier, a little smarter. I love going out there just because it's a little different; it's a new challenge—all part of constantly trying new approaches and keeping the business fresh.

Small changes can make a difference, too. You've got to be open to big changes, like the way I've kept changing the kind of merchandise we buy and sell, but you also don't want to ignore the small things. Think of little improvements you can do to keep things fresh, keep your business exciting. Recently I put new bright lights in our showcases to make the bling look even blingier. You can put lipstick on a pig and, certainly, it's still a pig, but people will look at it and think, *Hm, that's a cute pig.*

Whatever business you're in, I believe you should always be looking for ways to change proactively rather than having change forced on you. You'll make your customer happier, and you'll keep yourself happier, too. You don't have to own your own business to push for change in your work. You can change yourself and your own performance; at the end of every day, while you're sitting on the couch watching TV, think about how your day went and what you can do better tomorrow. Even better, start making those changes now instead of sitting on the couch watching TV! Read up on your industry and your company's place in it, and figure out something you can do to help the company move forward. If you're a marketer for a small business, for example, get on the Internet and see what the bloggers are saying about your industry and what changes might be coming your way. That's just one way you can stay ahead of your competitors. Learn to embrace change, and you'll learn to love your job.

Build a Culture of Change

I love getting suggestions from my employees. Sometimes they have ideas for better mousetraps. Sometimes they're smarter than me. It's the same with my kids. They've got great ideas, too. It's easy to look at your kids and think they're still seven years old. But I value any kind of change they can bring to the store, and I want them to help me take our business to the next level.

Seth has persuaded me to try Internet sales. The Internet business has thrived under Seth, growing to 15 percent of our total sales.

I want the same from my employees. Every single one of my managers started out at the bottom of the company, moving TVs around in the warehouse or doing similar grunt work. The employees who had ideas, who showed me a spark of passion for the business, have advanced. Not everybody can be a leader. Some of us are always going to be followers. So when I'm looking for someone to promote, I'm looking for someone who has that spark, who believes she's headed for something bigger.

I've always listened to feedback and ideas from my employees. Way back when I first opened American Jewelry and Loan, my employee Paul suggested we hire a jewelry repairman. He reasoned that it would make our store more of a destination for jewelry buyers and owners. His one suggestion was an important foundation for our ongoing success.

If you work for a business where your ideas aren't welcome, I feel for you. Back when I worked for my dad, he was dead set against pretty much every idea I ever had. I wanted to take Sam's Loan out of the 1940s to the modern day. My dad basically wanted to leave everything the way it was. We used to sell pretty low-quality merchandise. Our display cases were full of gold-filled rings (where the gold is mixed with a cheaper metal like brass or is gold plated) and cubic zirconia. I said, "Let's put at least one solid-gold chain in the showcase. Show our customers that we've got high-quality goods for sale." But my dad was afraid of thieves and refused to display any real gold. He was probably also afraid of being challenged by me—and of having my idea work. I did drag that store into the 1960s eventually, but it was step by painful step.

Maybe with some difficult bosses, persistence and diplomacy will work, and eventually you'll get them to accept your ideas. But some people are just never going to listen. They're always going to feel that an idea that comes from someone else is a threat to their position as top dog. If you've got a boss like that, all you can do is hold on to your ideas. Keep thinking and brainstorming ways to make your job and your business better. Don't let that jerk take your passion and creativity away from you. Save up those ideas and you'll have a lot to talk about when you get a chance to interview for a new job. You don't have to stay at a dead-end job forever. Go where you're appreciated.

Every Business Has Its Stories

It's not just the variety that makes me fall in love with my job every day. It's also the way my job puts me in touch with all kinds of people, with all their weird, challenging, ridiculous, moving stories. I know firsthand that in any job where you're interacting with the public, you're never going to be bored. Not only do I never know what kinds of items are going to be walked through my door, I never know what kinds of people I'll be talking to and what kinds of stories I'll hear.

To be honest, a lot of those stories are bullshit. There is no place in the world where you'll hear more bullshit than at a pawnshop. You think you've heard it all, and then somebody comes in with something totally off the wall, like the guys who want to pass off obviously fake artworks as the originals. But I love that part of pawn-broking, too. Every interaction with a customer, every deal, becomes a challenge. I've got to figure out *Is this person telling me the truth? Is he trying to pull the wool over my eyes? Does he think he's smarter than I am?* I'm sixty-two years old, I've heard thousands of stories, and I'm pretty skeptical at this point, but I still get a kick out of interacting with somebody who thinks he's putting something over on me. If its elaborate enough, it becomes a game: Is he going to get away with this?

Some people get away with their tall tales. Not many—I think I'm pretty good at spotting bullshitters by now—but every once in a while someone does take me in. Two kids came in recently with some sports memorabilia, including a shirt signed by three Detroit Red Wings players. They wanted to do a straight sale, and the merchandise was decent, so we gave them $125 for it. The very next day a man came into the store and said his stepson had stolen the merchandise and sold it out from under him. He told us we needed to give it back to him. Well, how was I to judge between the two parties? I told him, "I can't do that unless I see a police report."

In that case, the owner did bring in the report and I returned the merchandise to him.

Having a TV show has only attracted more bullshitters. Now people come in who are on a mission to fool Les. The other day a customer came in with an old boat compass. He claimed it was a Baker Compass Company piece and worth $300. It looked valuable: It was mounted on a piece of beautifully finished maple wood, it had brass fittings, and was made, apparently, in the 1940s. But just to be sure—as I do with anything I'm not familiar with—I went into the back and looked it up online. It turned out that the compass was not worth nearly as much as he was asking for. There was a seller online who lived literally a mile from my store selling one of these things for $33. I went back out to the floor and said to this customer, "Do you think I'm an idiot? Do you think I'm not going to look this up?"

Because of the show and because people want to beat me at my own game, I need to keep getting better and better at spotting fakes and ruses. I have to learn more and more about pricing and counterfeiting, too. Fooling me is a contest for some people. I hope they realize it's a game for me, too. I don't like being fooled, but I do like a challenge.

Love Your Customers

Not all of the stories I hear are lies. Day after day people walk into my store genuinely in need, and I can help them—and I love that. It's not always just about making the deal; sometimes it's about helping people out. Even in the darkest days when the store was struggling, I loved going into work because I could help solve problems for people.

My typical 8 Mile customer isn't looking for a $25,000 loan. She's not starting a small business or putting a down payment on a house. My customer is usually just trying to scrape by and support a family. I believe it's part of my job to help her to do exactly that. I remember one woman who came in looking for a small loan to help cover burial expenses for her father. Now I've heard thousands of stories, so I think I'm pretty good at spotting the truth. I believed this woman, and I gave her more money than her item was worth because I could see she really needed it. She came back in the next day with the death certificate just to prove to me that she was telling the truth. I gave her $50 out of my own pocket.

Another customer came in recently with a bunch of sports memorabilia. He needed to raise money to go down south to rescue his daughter, who was being abused by her stepfather. He was desperate for cash, and he said he wanted a couple thousand dollars for his stuff; I had to tell him that he couldn't expect to get the kind of money people are asking for on eBay. A lot of people make that mistake—the price you see when you look at an item on eBay is the asking price. If you want to know what something's really worth, you have to find the final sale price. I could only offer this guy $500 for his items, or else the store would be losing money on the deal. He had actually stopped by the shop on his way to the airport and he was desperate, so he took the deal. His story and dedication really affected me. I said to him, "I'm going to reach into my pocket and give you a gift to make sure you've got enough cash to do what you need to do. Because the store will be OK, but I want you to be able to get your daughter." I gave him a $100 bill. He put that money in his pocket and he started to cry.

Even *Hardcore Pawn* seems to be helping people. I was in New Orleans recently with Lili and she wanted me to buy her one of those famous doughnuts they have there, the beignets. While I was in line to get the beignets, a kid came up to me and asked if he could get his picture taken with me. He told me he was taking a marketing class and that his professor made the students watch our show in class to learn about negotiations. If you had told me ten years ago that what I did every day in my pawnshop would be taught in a college class, I never would have believed you. But I've learned that even sharing the store's ups and downs on TV has helped people.

Almost every business ultimately exists to help people. If you can focus on that, and remember to personally connect to your work and your customers or clients, it'll help you stay passionate about what you're doing. Focus on the moments when you connect with another person, not on the nasty e-mail you just got or the boring meeting you just sat through. If you can find ways to focus on connecting with people, you'll learn to love your work.

Commit to Making the Effort

Another piece of the passion puzzle is commitment. If you commit to making an effort at your job, you'll love going to work because you'll be able to take genuine pride in what you're doing. Every day you go to work, no matter what business you're in or where you are on the company totem pole, strive to be better than you were yesterday.

Easily, the best employee I have is my janitor, Larry. I first met him when he came into the shop to sell some jewelry. He was homeless and had nothing to his name other than the jewelry, really. He brought in a bracelet and asked $20 for it. I ended up giving him $200 because he hadn't realized the piece had gold in it.

I can say without hesitation that I changed Larry's life. But he's also changed mine—and changed the attitude of every person he interacts with in the shop. He takes such pride in the work that he does, cleaning the bathrooms and the parking lot, I only wish I could get some of my other employees to share that attitude. I tell him that all the time. You never see him just sitting around except when he's on a scheduled break. I believe Larry's example proves that you can find something to be passionate about and proud of in any kind of work you're doing.

When you're committed to the job you're doing, you work harder than the next person. And sometimes it's not just commitment to the job at hand, but commitment to expanding your horizons and network for the future. I recently had dinner with a friend of a friend, a lawyer who wanted to meet me because he was trying to make more connections in Detroit. Immediately after we sat down to dinner, it became obvious that he had taken the time to research me online. He knew about my history, the current state of our business, and all about the TV show. It was pretty impressive—just that bit of extra effort made him stand out from all the other people I'd met recently.

How badly do you want to succeed? You need to drive yourself to do better than the person in the cubicle next to you. Even if you don't love what you're doing at a given moment, even if you don't think the job is the right one for you, you have to find a way to commit to making the effort and doing the best you can. It's the only way you'll advance in the job or move on to a better one in the future. Taking any job is a choice you made and every job on earth offers an opportunity to learn and grow. But you have to be committed to the job at hand. When I hire somebody new and he starts as a stock guy moving TVs around in the back of the warehouse, he may feel he'd rather be working out front selling jewelry on the floor. But he's not going to get there right away. He's got to show me some commitment first.

Commitment First, Love Later

If you don't feel passionate about your job right now, take a harder look at what you're doing. Is there some part of your job that you do love? Is there something you love that you can bring into what you're doing? In most jobs you're never going to get out of the warehouse and into the position that looks more exciting if you don't find some passion first. That passion has to come from within you. You can't wait for the world to hand you the most fascinating job ever. You've got to commit yourself to find the drive and routine first. That will push you forward into a career that you will learn to love.

At this point in my life I could retire and live comfortably. But do I want to? Heck no. In my mind, I'm still a twenty-five-year-old guy striving to be successful. That will never change. The rest of me is a bit older, but between my ears I'll always be a kid trying to prove myself. I'm committed to my job—and just about everything else I do, too. It's one of the reasons I like to work out every day. At sixty-two years old, I'm still bench-pressing. When I spin, I spin for an hour and two minutes. Why? Because anybody can spin for an hour. And if they can do it for an hour, I can do it a little longer than they can, for an hour and two minutes.

Working out is how I prepare myself for my workday. Every morning I get out of bed, put on my gym clothes, and lift weights or spin. I push myself physically so I'm ready to push myself at work. Working out helps me focus on what I have to do next. I don't believe in just rolling out of bed and rushing into the office, drinking your coffee on the way. I believe you've got to prepare yourself for your day deliberately.

When we shoot the TV show, part of my preparation is to put on the white sweater I usually wear, and clip on the microphone. Before that, though, I've been mentally preparing myself while I get ready physically. It's a conscious, deliberate, repetitious routine that gets me psyched up to do what I do. You can't approach your work with passion if you're half asleep. Wake up, get ready, and get to work.

I know we're all working for a paycheck. Money motivates me, too. When I was younger, I was struggling to build a business so I could support my family. These days I'm fighting every day to make that business as strong as it can possibly be so that it'll support my kids' families and my employees' families. My business supports fifty-five families, and I never forget that. But if your paycheck is the *only* thing getting you out of bed in the morning, you've got a problem. After all, your paycheck depends on the passion you put into what you're doing. I'm just as excited when I close a twenty-dollar deal as when I close a deal for thousands of dollars because I love the thrill of the chase.

You have to do whatever it takes to keep your life and your work exciting. When it gets boring, you'll get complacent, you'll become passive, and you'll lose. If you embrace and seek out change in your work, find meaning in connecting with people, and commit to making the effort, you will learn to love your work. Being on a TV show, writing this book—I'm always looking for new challenges. Not knowing what's going to happen next makes it a thrill to wake up every morning.

CHAPTER 4

Build a Business with No Boundaries

A pawnshop is a place where you can find anything and everything. We're a car dealership,
we're Home Depot, we're Zales. We're whatever you need us to be. Some of our customers are desperate for cash, and others are ready to shell out $30,000
for a pair of diamond earrings. Growing up in this
shape-shifting industry taught me to take an expansive
view of what my business could be. I believe in building
a business with no boundaries. And you don't have to
own your business to take a no-boundaries attitude toward your career. In this chapter I'll show you why it's
important not to let yourself be limited by

+ **what you've always done;**
+ **what other people think you are;**
+ **what you think the rules are supposed to be; or**
+ **what conventional wisdom says you should do.**

Anything and Everything
Is Fair Game

In a pawnshop, anything and everything you could possibly want will eventually walk through the door. A few years ago, my wife, Lili, got a horse, and she needed a saddle. I put a sign in the window of the store that said, "We now buy saddles," and the next day, I bought three.

There's almost nothing I won't buy, as you've seen. As long as I know I can sell it, I'll buy it. I once bought a certified piece of Abe Lincoln's hair for $400. I'll buy dentures as long as there's gold in them. Of course, there are a few exceptions. An Iraq war vet came into the store the other day and wanted to pawn two rings for $40. We settled on $20. We got to talking and I asked him what happened to him in the war. He said, "I lost my eye"—and he popped his glass eye out of its socket! He asks me, "Can I pawn this?" and hands it to me.

I didn't take that glass eye. There's not much market for those things. But my business has thrived over the years because I think of it as a business with no boundaries. You can't keep those four walls the same way they always were. You can't be limited by what you've always done—that's fatal.

What Do I Need to Sell Today?

In a way, I'm lucky that I'm a pawnbroker because my business is a barometer of the entire economy. Pawnbrokers are economists at the street level. We know before the *Wall Street Journal* and *Forbes* how the economy is really doing. I get an early warning when the economic situation in the country is changing, and I can adjust what I have to do to keep money coming in.

Back in 2008, I could tell that the person on the street was in trouble. At American Jewelry and Loan we have two lines: the incoming pawn line, where people are bringing in merchandise to use as collateral to get a loan, and the redemption line, where people are coming in with cash to get their merchandise back. Usually the pawn line gets long in December, when people are getting ready for

Christmas, and then when people get a bonus or a tax refund, the redemption line picks up early in the new year.

After the New Year, though, we had a huge pawn line, and this held true through 2012. Normally our redemption rate is about 85 percent, which means that more than four out of five customers come back to redeem their possessions. By early 2009, our redemption rate dropped down to 65 percent and even as low as 50 percent during one brief period. In addition, we were seeing a lot more six-figure-income customers—people who usually wouldn't even think about walking through the door of a pawnshop—coming to both American Jewelry locations to pawn their possessions. They had lost their jobs, their homes were being foreclosed, and they had little or no money in the bank.

In certain ways my business was picking up, but it was all out of balance. I had tons of merchandise in inventory, including a lot of gold and diamonds, but the retail side of the business was dead. Nobody was buying expensive items. So I had to start thinking differently. We were still selling birthday gifts, engagement rings, holiday gifts—but at lower price points.

It was crucial, during this time, that I had enough cash on hand to keep my revenue up. My store is called American Jewelry and Loan, but it's the "and Loan" that really keeps the doors open. As soon as you stop making loans, you lose your customer. In the past I've sold my own jewelry, even my own watches, to raise some cash to keep making those loans. In 2008, with the retail side of my pawnshop going nowhere, I knew I had to do something to keep cash coming in. I couldn't let myself be limited to what I had always done.

I looked around at what I had in stock and realized I had an excess of the tiny stones known as melee diamonds. You often see them set around larger stones in jewelry, and dealers would frequently come into the store hoping to buy such small diamonds wholesale. I figured that I could take jewelry out of inventory, rip out the tiny diamonds, and resell them for $35 a carat. I was losing money on the melee diamonds, but I was raising the cash I needed for my business.

You've always got to be willing to change what you're doing. You can't be bound by the way things have always been. If the economy changes, if trends change, if your customer starts requesting something different, you've got to change your business response even if it means launching a completely new product or service.

This principle applies to individuals, too, whether or not you own a business. I can tell you, as an employer, that I never want to hear an employee say, "That's not in my job description" or "I've never done that before." You can't let yourself be limited by what you've always done. You have to be willing to experiment and try new things, whether that means redesigning a product line or taking on a new responsibility at work. Forget the past and focus on what you need to be doing today to make tomorrow successful.

Pushing Past Geographic Boundaries

In 1978, when I was twenty-eight and still working for my father, he started talking about opening a second store. I said to him, "You know what we need to do? Move to the suburbs. That's the way of the future." My dad believed that Dearborn would be the best place to expand, but I told him that was the wrong direction. Dearborn was too close to the city center where we'd always been located. I wanted to move north, closer to the nicer suburbs. Pawnshops had always been in the cities, but we were going to change that.

So I went to the landlord of a little shopping center in the suburb of Oak Park and made a deal for an old Sherwin-Williams paint store. It was a tiny, narrow shop, fifteen feet by one hundred feet, but it was in the right neighborhood—the neighborhood I grew up in. The landlord was nervous about renting to a pawnbroker, and he told me I should talk to the police. On his advice I went to the local police department and told the lieutenant that I was going to open a pawnshop in Oak Park. He laughed at me. But I looked him right in the eye, showed him that I was serious, and I got him to say he'd support me.

The next step was speaking to the Oak Park City Council. Although there was no law against opening a pawnshop in the suburbs, it had never been done before.

The support of the police department helped, but some of the folks on the council just didn't want a pawnshop in their neighborhood. They didn't see what I saw: that the business can change, that we could push past the boundaries of what a pawnshop has always been.

I received enough votes to get the license I needed, and that new store opened in January 1978. At that time, my father and I were partners, but three years later I left my dad's shop, separated our business interests, and went to work at the new store, American Jewelry and Loan, full-time. Back then, that store was writing about five to seven loans a day. There were three women working there at the time, and their desks were always piled high with magazines to help pass the time because business was so slow. It was a tiny operation compared to my grandfather's store.

But the day I took over, in March of 1981, I walked in and said, "Ladies, I'm here, and this store is never going to be the same again."

I'd walked away from a multimillion-dollar business and I was starting over with zero, with nothing but a total readiness to work hard. I was in that store every day, doing everything from washing the windows to making sales. I knew I could attract the suburban client base I wanted if I created the right kind of atmosphere. By August, we were making fifteen or twenty loans a day, and I hired a jewelry salesman. By December, I was ready to hire a jewelry repairman.

I would never have been able to build the business I have today if I'd been content to stay within the boundaries of other people's expectations. Even if every single person in the Detroit metro area thought of pawnshops as one particular thing, I had to be able to look past their opinion.

You can't let yourself be limited by what other people think you are—or should be. They don't know your business the way you do. They don't know *you* the way you do. They're not going to bother imagining new roles you could play. They're not going to take the time to think about how your business could change to fit into a new community. You've got to push past those boundaries on your own.

New Venture, New Vision

I always had my eye on the next big thing. That first store in Oak Park was just 1,500 square feet, but there was a restaurant in the same shopping center that was about 3,500 square feet. I was always looking for the next location, the next way to expand, so when that restaurant went out of business in 1983, I was ready to lease it. Not only did I want to move into that bigger space, I wanted to expand our merchandise. I wanted to add electronics. So I went back to the police department and told them I wanted to sell computers in my new space. By this time, they knew me, and it wasn't a problem.

Back to the city council I went, and this time they voted unanimously to allow me to open a new, bigger shop. They later approved me to take (and sell) rifles and shotguns—the first and last time they ever allowed the practice in Oak Park.

My business wouldn't be what it is today if I hadn't been willing to keep trying new things. I also had to be willing to listen to ideas from sources I wouldn't necessarily consider. Back in the early eighties I hired that first jeweler, Paul, for American Jewelry and Loan. Paul had previously worked in traditional jewelry stores, and he helped me see past the way pawnbrokers usually operate and come up with new ideas for the business. Paul told me we should hire somebody to do jewelry repair. I loved the idea. It was another way to get customers in the door, another source of revenue, and it was also a way to make the store feel different from a typical pawnshop. Once we had a repair person in the shop, we didn't just offer loans and great deals on somebody else's merchandise; we became a real destination for new and used jewelry.

I've been around jewelry all my life, so I think I've developed an eye for what looks good. As we developed the jewelry side of the business, I started to do more designing of my own. I'd had an interest in design ever since I was a kid selling those chains to department stores. I designed pieces for my mother, and I designed my wife's engagement ring. Now when customers come in looking for jewelry, I'm not limited to selling them just the pieces we have on hand. I can make them a custom piece with the stones we have in inventory.

A couple came in the store a few years ago looking for an engagement ring. They had already been to Jared's, and they had something in mind that they liked, but they wanted to shop around before making their final decision on a ring. Just by getting them in my front door, I'd proved the value of offering a more traditional jewelry store experience in the pawnshop. That small move proved we were competing with jewelry stores like Jared's. But, of course, I'm not going to settle for just getting the customer in the door. I always want to make the deal. I showed the couple an emerald-cut 2.75-carat diamond, a gorgeous stone, almost twice as big as the stone in the ring they were thinking about. I quoted them about half the price Jared's was going to charge them. I even told them I'd be able to make them a custom setting for the ring with smaller diamonds around it, similar to the design of the other ring but better because it was twice the stone for half the price. I was also able to show them another custom ring we had just made to prove that we knew what we were doing.

I made the sale and the ring turned out to be absolutely spectacular. The couple wouldn't have that ring today if I had let myself be limited only to what other people thought they wanted.

Still Expanding

Competing with the traditional jewelry stores at the mall means we're attracting a different kind of customer. We're dealing with the suburban shoppers I've been going after ever since I moved to Oak Park. As our customer changes, I also change the merchandise I buy and sell. I'm expanding beyond what you'll see at the typical pawnshop.

I used to buy sports memorabilia every now and then, not to sell but just to keep for my son, Seth. My daughter, Ashley, would inherit my wife's jewelry, so I wanted to have a few more personal items for Seth, too. Seth and I both love sports, so I thought it would be nice for him to inherit some stuff that has value but also might have some meaning for him. I never thought about trying to sell that kind of thing in the store until one day a customer arrived with some Mickey Mantle baseball cards. I was thinking about buying them for Seth, but one of my employees, Dennis, pulled me aside and whispered that he thought he could sell them for $300. He told me that the market for sports memorabilia that held sentimental value to fans is huge.

I never say no to a new way to make money, so I let Dennis try to sell this kind of memorabilia. He was right—he sold those baseball cards for $300, and we've since built up sports memorabilia into a big portion of our business. The back wall of the store used to be reserved for fur coats, but now, in the summer, we'll fill about 60 percent of that wall with such things as valuable baseball cards, signed balls, and game-worn jerseys—with the best-sellers, of course, being anything related to our hometown teams here in Detroit. I never would have thought I'd sell anything so far from the traditional pawnshop staples as a $1,000 Mickey Mantle baseball card or a $2,800 Honus Wagner card, but I was willing to try something new, and now we've got a whole new product line.

We haven't expanded only into sports items. We're selling many other new products to keep up with our new high-end customers. We've got Swarovski crystals, Lalique bottles and vases, and Mont Blanc pens. One customer brought in his liquor collection, and after a little research online, I figured out one of his bottles of Courvoisier was worth about $9,000. He knew he had something of value—he was asking for $15,000 for the whole collection. One of the bottles was actually a two-hundred-year-old brandy from Napoléon's collection, and I knew immediately that for that sort of incredibly rare find, the item's value only goes up as time passes because so few of those bottles exist. I bought the man's entire collection of liquor for $8,000.

I have never closed myself off from new business areas and new customers, and neither should you. Always be thinking about how you can change and improve what you're doing. Whether you offer to do more for your boss by, for example, volunteering to be in charge of updating your company's Facebook page or expanding your small flower shop, you can't just keep those four walls (mental or physical) the same. You've got to think beyond their boundaries. Currently Seth is working on building out our Web site, www.pawndetroit.com, to help us sell more American Jewelry and Loan items and *Hardcore Pawn* merchandise. Fans of the show can now buy T-shirts and hats and more through our Web site.

Like father, like son, Seth is now trying to build something even bigger, a new venture that goes beyond our physical pawnshop. He learned from me, after all. His idea is to build a site called Can I Pawn This? A user interested in pawning an item would go to the site and enter some information about the object, send us a photo of it, and someone from our staff would write back with an estimate of how much the seller could likely get for it. The site would then direct the seller to the nearest pawnshop. That way, if someone was a fan of our show but not based in Detroit, he could learn about another pawnshop where he could take the item.

I think Seth's idea is excellent. I told him I don't care how much he spends on this Web site as long as he ultimately makes a profit. I want him to learn to look at the business the way I do: choosing to take the pawnshop in different directions.

I believe you can approach any business this way. Not every business will change as radically as a pawnshop can, and does, but every business can expand beyond the boundaries that people outside it will see.

If you're not sure about where you need to take your business or how it needs to change, focus on your customer. What can you do to make her experience better? Where else does she shop? Is there a way you can bring the money she's spending somewhere else back into your store? I don't want my customer to pawn jewelry with me and then go somewhere else when she's in the market to buy a gold chain. I don't want someone to pawn her TV with me but go somewhere else to try to sell Grandma's antiques.

Ultimately I want my customer to share my vision. I want him to understand that my business isn't bound by the usual rules and to see that I'm flexible and willing to work with him to make sure he's happy. I want that customer to know I'm offering something different from the pawnshop down the street.

Beyond the Boundaries of Our Industry

I'll let you in on a little secret: Seth and Ashley didn't want to do the TV show at first. We met a producer because we held a Jerry Springer promotional event at our store in 2008, and the TV folks who came out to the event were impressed by how big and busy our store was. Then a few months later they approached us about doing a reality show. I was all for it. Lili was all for it. But Seth and Ashley and their spouses were dead set against it.

We talked about it for months. In a nice twist of fate, we got advice from a reality show pro. Lili and I went to a jewelry show around the time we were considering the TV deal, and we ran into Kris Jenner, the Kardashian matriarch, famous for being manager for her daughter Kim, and for her family's very popular reality show, *Keeping Up with the Kardashians*. Lili asked Kris what it was really like to be on a reality TV show. Kris told Lili that the experience is great, but you've got to be prepared to work hard—eighteen-hour days sometimes—and you've got to be prepared for your life to be an open book. That turned out to be pretty good advice.

Eventually we had a family meeting: Lili and I; Ashley and her husband, Jordan; Seth and his wife, Karen. I told them that I had a vision that doing the show could take us great places. I argued that it would grow our business and improve the image of the store. It wouldn't just change our own business; the show could change pawnbroking forever. We would be able to demonstrate to people that pawnshops are a legitimate business and reverse the stigma often associated with establishments like American Jewelry and Loan. I said, "I think it'll be great for us, and I intend to do it, with or without you." I guess that got their attention! My kids and their spouses agreed to do the show. They said, "If you're doing it, we're doing it with you. We've got to keep an eye on you. You're unpredictable!"

The first thing we shot for the show was something called a sizzle reel, which is essentially an eight-minute mini-pilot. With the camera trained on me, I stood in the front of my store and held up a pawn ticket. "This is a story," I said. "And there's forty thousand more in this building."

I think that's why our show has been successful: Our business, and our show, is as big and as varied as human nature is. Every single person who walks into our shop has a story composed of who they are, where they got the item they're pawning or selling, why they need the cash. There's no limit to the kinds of stories we can tell and, therefore, the kinds of things we can sell.

Ultimately my kids were right: I am unpredictable. It's not because I'm off the rails; it's because my *business* is always changing. It's always growing. Sure, some aspects of pawnbroking are never going to change. People always need cash. It's always the pawn business that keeps the store going. But I'm focused on making the pawnbroking experience different. I want the customer who walks through my front door to feel differently than he would in any other pawnshop in the world. The TV show has helped us change the image of our business tremendously. Instead of letting other people tell me what my business should be, I'm showing them what I believe it will be.

You can do the same thing as an individual. If you're in the business of building your own career, you've got to have this same expansive attitude. You can't let yourself be limited by what other people think you are. If you want to work directly with customers, but your boss thinks you're a perfect fit for the back-end role you have now, don't let that perception limit you. Find ways to show her you can succeed in the role you want. Volunteer to help a colleague with a project that will connect you with customers. Give a presentation at the next staff meeting to prove that you're personable and good on your feet. Don't let someone else tell you where your career is going. Show them where you want it to go.

Breaking the Rules

I try to teach my employees to have this anything-goes attitude, too. Sometimes it takes them a while to catch on. For example, the women at the jewelry-buying counter were trained to buy gold for a certain price under the current wholesale price. After a while I realized that they were letting customers walk out the door when they couldn't settle on the price I'd told them to go for. Now, I don't like to let anybody walk out my door without making a deal if I can help it. So I told the women I was changing the policy: If they think they need to buy gold at a higher price, they should ask a manager about it. Really, the price was always flexible, but my employees needed to be told they were allowed to break a rule they thought was set in stone.

If you focus on making sure your customer never walks out your door empty-handed, you'll find yourself doing whatever it takes to make that sale, even if it means doing something you've never done before. Recently I was in our warehouse, and a family came in hoping to buy a generator. We were selling one for $350 that would cost them $600 at Home Depot, but they were ready to walk out and go to the big-box store because they wanted a warranty.

On the spot, I decided to start offering warranties. I told them, "Give me an extra twenty-five dollars, and I'll give you a warranty for ninety days. If anything happens to this generator that isn't your fault, I'll replace it or give you your money back, no questions asked." We had never given a warranty on any item before—but I don't care about the way I ran things yesterday if I find a better solution today. I just didn't want a potential customer to do business with Home Depot instead of with me. If someone has money, I'd like them to give it to me. Providing that warranty helped us close the deal. My employee asked me, "Les, can I do this again if I need to? Am I allowed to give out warranties now?" "We do whatever the customer needs us to do," I said. "Period."

Obviously, we can't break all the rules. We've got to keep careful track of the loans we make and the items we take in pawn. We have to treat our customers with respect and encourage them to treat us with respect. Anything else we can do to satisfy the customer that doesn't touch the integrity of the business is fair game.

I think that applies to any business. Don't do anything that will undermine the integrity of your business, but be willing to do just about anything else. If you're running a restaurant or bakery and somebody asks if you do catering, say yes. If you're designing a Web site and someone asks if you can train their employees to do some basic coding, say yes.

The key to running a successful business is closing the deal. That's it. You've got to be able to make decisions on the fly, and you've got to teach your employees to do the same. Just close the deal. Don't let artificial boundaries cost you money. Don't let yourself be limited by what you think the rules are. The only boundaries on your business are the ones you set yourself.

Look for Ideas Everywhere

A no-boundaries attitude means looking for ideas anywhere and everywhere you can find them. After all, a great way to be different from your competitors is to look for ideas outside your own field. For example, in my store we've got five windows for people who are pawning jewelry and only one for picking it up, sometimes two if the redemption line gets backed up. So I stole an idea from fast food: Instead of having the clerk who took the customer's ticket go into the vault to look for his merchandise, now that clerk at the front can just enter the customer's information into the computer and ring a bell. Then one of the employees in the back will find the item and bring it out to the customer. The entire transaction shouldn't take more than five minutes. I figured if McDonald's could do it, why couldn't I?

To be different from your competitors, to create a better experience for your customers, look anywhere you can for great ideas to copy.

Here's another idea you can't afford to ignore: Do anything you can to streamline your business. We used to keep track of our layaway business on index cards that we filed by hand. Then, in 2012, Seth pushed me to computerize our system. I tend to be very wary of keeping customer information anywhere outside of my vault because I don't want it to be vulnerable to hackers or thieves. Seth basically went behind my back and figured out a way to create a computerized layaway system that would be secure and could be easily integrated with the way we already run our business. Talk about good ideas! Now that the system is up and running, it's turned out to be one of the best ideas we—or rather, Seth—have had. Putting all of that information in a simple database has really reduced the number of mistakes my employees make.

Whatever will improve your business, don't be afraid to do it—even if it's not your idea or it's an idea from outside your field. Don't let yourself be limited by what conventional wisdom says you should do. You can be bigger than the way things have always been done in your industry.

Where a Bigger Vision Will Take You

After changing our store and opening our doors to the TV cameras, I believe the public image of pawnbrokers has really started to change. These days it's cool to come to the pawnshop. I'm starting to see wealthier people there, and as a result, I'm making bigger loans. When we started filming *Hardcore Pawn,* I figured our viewers would be the same sort of people as our typical customers. But according to the data I've seen, our viewers actually make a good bit of money, and our customer base is starting to change, too. We've got big-time companies, such as Bud Light, advertising on our show now. One night in December of 2012, we were the biggest show on cable.

But I know it's not just the show, and it's not just my store—this change in customers and experiences is happening all over the country. Pawnbrokers from all over the United States are telling me that their businesses are changing, too. The business press is also catching on; I've read articles in *MarketWatch,* the *Financial Times,* and elsewhere about how pawnshops are bringing in higher-end customers who want the convenience and discretion we've always been known for. That wouldn't be possible if we hadn't changed what it means to walk into a pawnshop.

The other day a person came into our shop to tell me he'd just opened a pawnshop in North Carolina. He watches our show, and it made him want to get into the business; he said he couldn't pass through Detroit without coming to see the original American Jewelry and Loan. That's what I'm aiming for. I want pawnshops to be cool, sure, and I want our TV show to be popular, but more than that, I want pawnshops to be respected. I want people to see us as a legitimate business. If I hadn't seen that big picture—if I hadn't seen the ways my business needed to change to make it a better experience for my customers—I would still be a small-time pawnbroker.

[CHAPTER 5]

Negotiate Like a Pawnbroker

You may not think that buying and selling stripper poles and locks of dead presidents' hair has much to do with your business, but it does. Every business involves negotiation. No matter your job, you've got to be able to sell, whether you're selling a product, a service, an idea, or yourself. You also have to know how to buy, whether buying raw materials, services, or talent. I'm going to tell you the secrets I've learned from decades of deals. In this chapter, you'll learn

- ✦ **why you should never prejudge your customer;**
- ✦ **why a good salesperson is a good performer;**
- ✦ **how to stay focused on closing the deal;**
- ✦ **why you should add emotion to the equation when selling;**
- ✦ **why you should take emotion out when buying; and**
- ✦ **why you've got to remember that the worst you can hear is "No."**

Pawnbroking 101

I learned how to make a deal from watching Louie. Louie was the best salesman in my grandfather's pawnshop when I was growing up. He had been working there since about 1940. He didn't know how to run a business. In fact, he didn't really have a sense of how to make a business profitable. He had no sense of the big picture you need to run a business successfully, and I hate to say it, but he really wasn't very smart. Louie was what my grandparents would have called a *nebbish*, the kind of guy who would get hooked in the ear if he walked past a fishhook—a follower, not a leader.

What's worse, Louie was a thief. He was an old-fashioned guy and he always wore a hat, one of those fedoras, all day, every day. Eventually Popsie figured out he was stealing money from the till and hiding it in his hat. Popsie didn't fire Louie; he just made him stop wearing the hat. He was too good a salesman to let go, which tells you something important about Popsie. He *did* get the big picture—which was why he realized it made sense to keep Louie on, selling every day, even if he skimmed a little off the top of his deals.

Because Louie could sell. Louie could sell anything. He closed more deals than Popsie, my father, and me combined, day in, day out. Watching Louie in action was like taking Pawnbroking 101. He was the best salesman I've ever known. Louie continued working for my father at Popsie's pawnshop until L.G. fired him in 1985, after Popsie was gone. L.G. was not a big-picture thinker, and he didn't like Louie. I think Louie's presence reminded him of Popsie, a man he could never measure up to.

So Louie came to me at American Jewelry and Loan for a job and I hired him on the spot. It was a great move for me and the store. He worked for me until he retired a dozen years later.

Louie had a unique style of selling, and you couldn't learn it anywhere else. He broke pretty much all of the classic rules of salesmanship. Never a very self-confident person, Louie rarely made eye contact with the customer. To make matters worse, he also talked too much. Having been in this business as long as I have, I know how important it is to listen to your customer, but Louie would never shut his mouth. Sometimes it seemed that people would buy something from him just to shut him up.

My own selling techniques are slightly different—for instance, I look people in the eye these days—but Louie taught me a few really important lessons. The biggest secret to his success was that he knew how to talk. Sure, he might take it too far sometimes, not even quitting the talk after he had won the sale, but he did have the gift of gab. He was extremely convincing. Although he might not know the first thing about whatever he was selling, listening to him, you'd think he was an expert because he knew how to sound sure of himself and what he was saying. Most of all, he knew how to tell the customers what they wanted to hear.

Louie's real strength was focusing on the emotional truth of what the customer needed. Some people may call this bullshit, but I think it's one of the most important sales tactics. If you figure out an emotional truth, you can tell the customer what it will mean to him to own the item. For example, let's say you want to sell a particular sweater to a customer. Don't talk up the sweater itself. Tell the customer that he'll look distinguished in it or fashionable or manly. A good salesperson figures out what button to push by sizing up the customer.

I once watched a glass salesman go to work on a potential customer who had his family with him. The salesman tried prestige, telling him how this was the world's best glass, and he'd be the envy of his friends if he bought some. No go. Then he tried luxury, telling him that this was the world's most expensive glass, and it said something about the potential buyer that he could afford it. Still no go. He tried appealing to his love of his family, saying that he owed it to his wife and daughter to get them this beautiful glass. Nothing. Finally, he tried the heirloom approach, telling the potential customer that the glass would become a treasured family possession that he could hand down to his children and they to their children.

Bingo. Soon the customer was writing a $2,000 check. The glass hadn't changed, but the emotional truth of the meaning of the glass to the customer had changed—the salesman had found his mark.

If you tell that truth as powerfully as that glass salesman or Louie could, you'll find it's much more important to the customer than the details of how the item works or how much its resale value is or whatever its features are. Louie almost never knew any of those details, but he always knew what kind of story he was telling about the item he was selling and how it was going to change the customer's life.

Don't Judge Your Customer

I think that some of Louie's success at spinning those stories came because he wasn't the most confident person or the smartest or the luckiest. In this way, no matter who walked into the store, Louie could relate to that person. He was the instant equal of every customer and made customers feel that they were on the same level.

I still follow his example in treating the whole range of my customers as my equals. When I walk into my store, I become like my customers. I wear a big diamond earring in my ear because that's what I'm selling. I put on a tough-guy attitude because that's the culture my basic customer in the 8 Mile store comes from. I relate to them the way I saw Louie relate to the customers at Sam's Loan. Whoever walks in my door, I want them to feel that I'm no different from them. And I've found that my more upscale customers like the sense that they're seeing a different slice of life, in a safe environment, so it doesn't hurt to keep the tough-guy image!

You can't judge your customers before you speak to them. You can't size up people on sight; you have to take the time to talk to them and get a feel for who they are. I proved that at a car dealership once. When I was in my early thirties, Lili and I were in the market for a car. We decided to walk to a dealership that was close to our house. I was wearing blue jeans, and on the way to the lot, I fell into a hole on the side of the road that had been dug for a streetlight pole. My jeans got drenched. I walked into the dealership with soaking-wet pants and looking quite young. Needless to say, to the guys on the lot, I did *not* look like I was ready to drop a lot of money on a new car.

But I was ready to buy a car. As soon as we walked in, I set eyes on a beautiful silver Corvette. It was the car I'd dreamed of my whole life, without ever knowing I was dreaming of it. The salesman who had been dealing with me and Lili quoted me $30,000. Because I'm a deal maker, I figured I could negotiate a bit. I told him, "I'm going to give you $25,000 and trade in my old Datsun." Even though the price I threw back at him was going to cut into his commission, he said, "Sure." He took a chance on me—but he covered himself by turning around and betting his manager that I'd be back. His manager had already judged me in my soaking-wet blue jeans and decided I wasn't a serious buyer, so he took the bet.

Of course, I did come back. I went home, changed out of my jeans, and brought the Datsun in for the trade-in. The salesman lost his commission, but he made his money back with that bet. In the end, the sales manager who'd bet against me because of my appearance was the one who lost out. I can't imagine how angry he must have been that I'd come back when he thought I was a cheap punk. It just goes to prove that you shouldn't make assumptions about people until you talk to them.

I'm not saying that you should never draw any conclusions about a person. Separating the scam artists from the people in genuine need is a huge part of my job. And it comes down to instinct. I've seen so many deals that I can size up a person pretty quickly. I'm not always right, of course, but there's something about a scam artist who's trying a little too hard to seem reasonable that tips me off. And thieves are usually wired with adrenaline. The first group makes eye contact too conspicuously, and the second rarely looks you in the eye at all.

While I probably see more outright liars in my line of work than most people do, figuring out whom to trust is important in any industry. Making judgments about the people you deal with is acceptable as long as you spend some time getting to the bottom of their story first.

Never judge someone by the way they look. I can guarantee that if you walked into my store and tried to guess who among my customers was desperate for a $100 loan and who was ready to pay thousands of dollars for a piece of jewelry, you'd be wrong at least half the time. All you can tell from people's clothes is where they bought them. You don't know anything about their priorities, what they scrimp and splurge on, or what they've been saving up for. If you want to succeed as a deal maker, never judge your customer on first sight. Learn from Louie—try to relate to them.

A Good Salesman Is a Good Performer

A big part of being a good salesman is being a good performer. Before I landed the TV show, I was already sort of an actor because I was a salesman. Every day when I walk into my store, I play the part of Les the pawnbroker. He's a little different from Les the family man or Les the regular guy. He's tough as nails. He'll scream at you if he needs to. I can always cut that off and switch gears as soon as I need to. I think that comes from being a Gemini—I've got two sides to my personality. Even if I'm ranting and raving at someone who's trying to take advantage of me, I'm always aware of how I'm behaving and why. It's not fake; it's just that we all play a variety of roles throughout the day. You do the same as you go from family to friends to work and back home again.

Every salesman has to be able to put on a performance. It's a role you learn to play. Just like Louie would do, talking a mile a minute and making you feel he was your best friend. Whatever's happening in your personal life, you've got to learn to put that aside when you're talking to your customer. You smile when you're sad. If you have a bad day, you can't bring it to work. If you fought with your spouse, you put that aside when you walk out on the floor. The customers don't want to see your personal life playing out when you're speaking to them. You need to focus on their feelings, not yours. It's guaranteed—every time you're in a bad mood and you let it show, you'll sell less.

A customer came into the store recently and tried to sell me an antique truck. It was a 1955 Ford F-100, red and yellow—a really cool find if you're into that sort of thing. The customer asked $19,500 for it, which was just way too much. It was worth about $5,000. So I said no. Sometimes you're so far apart that you can tell you're not going to close the distance; and the seller is not going to go away happy, because he has an unrealistic idea of the value of his item.

Then this seller started getting mad at me! "Hold on now, I'm the buyer here," I said. "You can't get mad at me."

I added, "What do you do for a living? Because I can see you're not a salesperson."

That really put him over the edge. He lost his temper and shouted, "Hey, if you don't want to buy it, don't buy it." He also included a few other choice words.

I threw him out of the store. Who needs that kind of aggravation from a jerk? He bothered me—no sense of what sales is all about. You can't sell anything to anybody if you let them see you're in a bad mood. You've got to put on your salesperson act.

But that performance can't be totally fake. That was part of Louie's gift; even when he was spinning a story, he could find the emotional truth at its core. I got a good reminder of this the first day we started shooting *Hardcore Pawn*. When the cameras started rolling on that first day, I put on a new act, a character I thought would make sense for the TV show. I thought people would want to see a kinder, gentler pawnbroker—Les

LEFT: Popsie, my grandfather, was my protector, confidant, and biggest inspiration.

BELOW: My family in their early days in America. Popsie is fourth from the right in the back row, with his wife (my Bubbie) next to him, third from the right. My mom is the second from the right in the bottom row.

My Popsie and Bubbie helped out our family in any way they could. They're one of the reasons I value my own family relationships so much. TOP ROW, LEFT TO RIGHT: my father, L.G., Bubbie, Popsie, and my mother. My sister and I are pictured in the bottom row.

I wasn't always the best student—I preferred to be at the pawnshop or out selling my jewelry instead of at school—but I did try. Here I am in my high school graduation photo.

After my tough childhood, I wanted to make sure I was the best possible father to my kids. It must have worked, since they both work with me now!

LEFT: At daughter Ashley's bat mitzvah with my wife, Lili, and son, Seth.

ABOVE: The family on vacation together in Switzerland.

Striking out on my own was hard work, but I wouldn't have it any other way. Luckily, I had good people working with me, including Popsie's best salesman, Louie (Louie Kanarek). He's pictured in the polo shirt, probably preparing to close a deal.

With American Jewelry and Loan I quickly learned the value of having a family business—the way I wanted it. Pictured here are my sister-in-law Esther, my wife, Lili, and my mother-in-law, Mary, hard at work behind the counter at American Jewelry and Loan.

The American Jewelry and Loan storefront today. We're currently located in a fifty-thousand-square-foot former bowling alley. We've come a long way from when I first opened my shop in a tiny fifteen-hundred-square-foot space in a strip mall.

We've definitely got a lot in pawn and for sale in our shop. A quick tour includes guitars . . .

Jewelry...

Furs...

And sports
memorabilia.

We own unusual items, including the van used by Dr. Death (Dr. Jack Kevorkian, a prominent figure in Detroit history).

Known as Les's Lion, this taxidermy beauty stands tall in my office.

Of course, American Jewelry and Loan would be nothing without the fantastic people that work here. LEFT: Larry Caudie, for example. He's our janitor and one of the best employees, who always takes pride in his work. RIGHT: Brian Lattin. I've known him since he was sixteen, and he's become a huge asset to our business—and like family to me.

Jeff West, my jewelry repairman, is another key member of our team. He's been working with me for twenty-seven years and he's been a huge part of how we've grown this business, because he understands my vision for what a pawnshop can be.

Don Prahl (left) and Rodney Ridley (right) are two smart, aggressive, hardworking employees who help me manage American Jewelry and Loan.

At the end of the day, it's all about preserving the legacy. I'm working to make sure that American Jewelry and Loan is around for future generations to enjoy.

Gold cleaned up for the folks at home. I wasn't as aggressive as I would usually be. I smiled, I was cordial, I said, "Welcome to my pawnshop, I'm delighted to have you here."

Well, the computer deal I was trying to make went south. I couldn't close the deal without being Les Gold the pawnbroker, the person I am in the store every day. The producer and Seth called me out into the hallway and asked me what the heck was wrong with me. "You're acting," they said. "We want you to be you!"

Ever since, I've just been myself for the cameras. The version of myself that's a tough negotiator, anyway!

It takes some time to get comfortable with this idea of performance, but it's the key to becoming a great salesperson. You put on an act in the sense that you're putting your personal life aside in trying to relate to a total stranger—but you've also got to be genuine. People will spot it right away if you're being fake with them. You're not performing like you're on Broadway; you're performing like you're being the best or most confident version of yourself. A good salesperson puts on a performance— that best version of herself—so assuming you're not Daniel Day-Lewis or Meryl Streep, keep it simple. Don't try to play Macbeth, just play yourself on a good day, feeling friendly and confident.

· · ·

Close the Deal

Another important lesson I learned from Louie was to close the deal. Close the deal, no matter what. Louie didn't really care that much about the price in the end; he let Popsie worry about that. Louie just wanted to make the deal. Of course, back then at Sam's Loan we weren't dealing with much merchandise that had a lot of intrinsic value. We bought things cheap so we could sell things cheap, which was the original pawnbroker theory.

Louie always kept one thing in the forefront of his mind: *This person I'm talking to, she walked in here to buy something. She didn't come here just to say hello. She came here to give me some money.*

That's especially true in a pawnshop. These days some people do come into our shop just to look around, because now that we're on TV, we're a tourist attraction. For the most part, though, people don't go to a pawnshop to browse. They're there because they need something—either merchandise or cash—and they know they can get it from me at a good price. You can't close every deal, but we expect to close 90 percent of them.

Not every business has that kind of hit rate, of course. In many retail situations, you're working with people who really are just browsing or who don't really know what they want or who are shopping around comparing prices. Closing the deal also differs from industry to industry: If you're a computer tech, for example, you may measure a "closed deal" differently than I do. But I think the assumption that Louie always made, that the customer you're dealing with is with you to make a deal, will give you confidence either way. It is possible to be too aggressive when you're trying to close a deal, but assuming that a deal is possible, that it's the most likely outcome of your conversation, should keep you from hanging back too much and letting that deal slip through your fingers. If you assume the person you're talking to wants to buy, it'll help you stay focused on closing the deal.

Tell the Emotional Story

If you want to sell something, you need to add emotion to the equation. You need to inject the emotional truth that is at the heart of every interaction. And you need to convey that with a story. You want the customer to feel that you believe he or she is special. Don't judge your customers. Convince them that you have the best product around, and you're giving them the best service that there is.

After you've established a connection to the person, you want to get them excited about the product itself. It doesn't matter what it is—when you're selling it, it's the most beautiful, rare, and precious thing in the world. Talk it up, but focus on the emotion, not the features. You can get to the features later, when you're ready to close the deal.

Let's say someone comes into the store looking for a fridge. Connect with them in some way—food might be a good bet. Then you might talk about a memory of baking cookies with your grandmother or sharing a late-night snack with your dad—depending on how you size up the customer. A fridge in this way becomes a center of the home, a place to go for connection and joy. That's how you bring the emotions into the equation.

Initially most people don't really consider buying a Mac laptop only because it has the features they need at the best price. They consider that product because it's beautiful to look at it, and owning it makes them feel sophisticated and cool. That's the kind of feeling you want to evoke in a buyer. Think about how ads work. An ad for a Lexus might list some of the features of the car, but mostly it's trying to make you feel something— the speed, the grace, and the freedom a car can offer you. If all it did was list features, it wouldn't be a very good ad.

In order to draw that emotion out in your buyer—a desire for freedom, a love of luxury, a sense of new possibility, whatever the feeling might be—you have to put your own feelings aside. When I'm selling something, I try to forget all about what I paid for it or what I think of it. My goal is to put myself in the customer's shoes, understand what the item might mean to him or her, and sell it based on those feelings, not mine.

One day a customer came into the store with a pencil drawing of Michael Jackson. He had drawn it himself, and it was a pretty good illustration. But he wanted $5,000 for it—way too much, in my opinion. He told me he had been showing the work at a gallery for $10,000. So that's what he wanted to sell it to me for. Well, that didn't mean anything to me. People actually make this mistake a lot—they confuse an asking price for what something is actually worth. They'll come in with a watch and say they've just seen a similar one selling for $500 on eBay. But has anyone actually paid that much for it? Or is that just what the person hopes to get? There's a big difference.

Anyway, I liked the picture enough and was intrigued by what I might get it for. "Sell it to me," I said to the artist. "Convince me that I need to buy this from you."

He thought for a minute and then said, "It took me a really long time to do this."

Well, I couldn't care less about that! He was focusing on *his* feelings about the drawing, not mine. This is a pawnshop, not your parents' refrigerator door. I'm not going to buy it because it's important to you. You need to convince me it's important to *me*.

I told the budding artist that I couldn't possibly pay him anything like $5,000 for his drawing. He was about to walk out the door, disappointed, but as he headed for the exit, I noticed a couple pushing a stroller who were checking out the drawing. They looked interested. I stopped the artist and this couple, and I started selling the drawing to them. I talked about the legendary King of Pop and how this was a one-of-a-kind piece by a local artist. I focused on how owning this drawing would enrich their lives by making them sophisticated art patrons, and how it was a celebration of one of their favorite artists. I was totally focused on making the pitch all about them and how they felt.

In four minutes I sold that random pencil drawing for $3,500 to the couple. Both parties were thrilled.

If you can make an emotional connection to your customer, you can sell anything. Back at Sam's Loan, Louie could sell a radio to somebody who walked in wanting a TV. He would find out that they wanted to watch the baseball games on TV, and he would tell them that the announcers were better on the radio because they could make you see the game! And he would connect that to nostalgia about old-time baseball. If you don't have the exact thing the customers think they want, you can try to use your focus on the emotion of the situation to convince them that they want the thing you have.

Again, it's not bullshit. It's using your powers of persuasion to steer a customer away from the details to the big picture. By focusing their attention on the emotional truth of what they're looking for, you can help them believe the item you're selling them answers that emotional need.

If you can add emotion to the equation for the potential customer, selling is easy. Years ago, there was a guy—we'll call him George—who used to sell me my Yellow Pages ads. He moved to Florida a few years ago, but when, at the age of sixty-three, George got engaged, he and his fiancée came all the way up to Detroit to buy an engagement ring from me. He knew I would give him a fair deal. Now, these two had a pretty specific idea of what they wanted. George wanted to buy a three-carat diamond, and he wanted to pay around $20,000 for the ring. His fiancée had her heart set on a princess-cut stone—that's an elegant square shape that's very popular for engagement rings.

Unfortunately, I didn't have a three-carat princess-cut stone in the store at the time. I had a smaller princess-cut stone that had recently come out of pawn, and I had a five-carat pear-shaped diamond set in a simple ring that a friend had sold me after his mother died. A pear-shaped diamond is more of a teardrop shape, so it was a very different look but also a beautiful stone. It was larger than the diamond she thought she wanted. I had her try it on.

I knew that once she had that rock on her finger, she would never want to take it off. Having her try the ring on brought emotion into her buying experience. Once it was on her finger, she was no longer just thinking about cut, color, and clarity. She was thinking about what it would feel like to look down at her finger and see that beautiful stone, and how great it would be to show the ring off to her friends, or her mom. It didn't hurt the emotional story that her fiancé knew I wanted them to end up with a ring they loved at a good value.

I sold them that pear-shaped diamond for $32,000 after we agreed on a deal (for a diamond size they didn't know they wanted and $12,000 more than the budget they had in mind). While they stepped out for lunch, I reset the ring they wanted. Good, fast, friendly service also helps the buyers stay focused on how they feel about the item they're buying. You want to limit the amount of time the buyers have to come up with second thoughts.

I know selling that pear-shaped diamond was a good deal for me, and although that couple didn't buy the exact thing they had in mind, I got them a great deal on a gorgeous ring they're going to love for the rest of their lives. By focusing on the emotional connection, I was able to sell them the piece of jewelry I had even though it wasn't what they thought they wanted. That's why you should add emotion to the equation when you're selling—because it'll help you connect with your customer and persuade her she wants the item you're selling.

. . .

Forget Your Feelings When Buying

The customer who bought the engagement ring was an old friend of mine and I genuinely wanted to make him and his fiancée happy. Selling is all about tapping into the emotion. But in order to be a savvy buyer, you've got to be on your guard against the person who's trying to sell you something. You've got to take emotions out of the equation and focus on whether the item is worth the price. This is the flip side of the negotiation.

It's not easy. Even with as many deals I've made in a lifetime as a pawnbroker, I still have my weaknesses. Antiques, especially old drugstore signs, are one of my soft spots. A while back a customer came in with a beautiful example, a drugstore sign for a store long since out of business, in absolutely perfect condition, and I wanted it pretty badly. But he was asking $2,000 for it, and that was just too much to pay. I offered $1,200, and then $1,500, but he wouldn't take the deal. I let him walk away, but honestly, I still wish I had that sign.

The important thing is to keep your bottom line in mind. Is the person offering a price you can accept or not? For me, I have to focus on the item's resale value. It's pretty simple: I've got to be able to buy an item for less than I can sell it. For some items, including gold, there's a clearly established world marketplace and price listed on the Internet and on TV every day—but I still negotiate. To evaluate what other items are worth, I use a mix of experience, observation, and instinct.

I've been doing this for a while, so I have a pretty good sense of how much I can get for a lot of things. I also keep my eyes and ears open all the time for information about the price of just about anything under the sun. When I was younger, that meant walking into stores and examining price tags or picking up the newspaper and looking at Kmart's latest sales prices. Now we can look up merchandise online, but I've still made some great deals based just on stray bits of information I've picked up along the way. I've got a gold statue of a tiger on my desk that I was able to buy for much less than it was worth just because I happened to remember I'd once heard someone mention the artist's name. So I knew it was valuable, and I could offer a little more than I would have based on the gold alone.

Sometimes I really do just work on instinct. A customer came into the shop with a huge set of scales made of brass and steel. I had no idea what you'd use it for, but because I had never seen anything like it, I figured it was pretty rare. The customer wanted $300 for it, so I offered him $100. I threw in a little additional persuasion to close the deal, and convinced him that there was nobody else out there who would want to buy it. Clearly, I was giving him the best deal he was going to get. We made a deal and I found myself with the scales, not quite sure how to resell them.

Not long after, in walked a customer whose job was disassembling factories when they closed. Apparently, he had been looking for a set of scales like this his whole life. I talked that gentleman into buying this item from me. He was very happy and so was I. It might have been partly luck, but I closed that sale both times because I was able to trust my gut. I negotiated without emotion on the buy side; then I added the emotion back in when a customer came in who obviously cared about those scales.

I switch in and out of those two modes all day, every day. When I bought the set of scales, I looked at it purely as a commodity. In this case that was easy, because I wasn't exactly emotionally attached to the deal. But when I sold it, I was able to put the emotion back in to close my sale. I saw how excited the customer was to find this set of scales, how it was going to make his job easier and generally improve his life, and so I talked up that aspect of the deal. I emphasized how good it would look in his office. I put the emotion back into the equation when it was to my advantage.

I'm not perfect; I make some bad deals, too. When the kids were younger, I took the whole family on a trip to Russia. As I was on my way to change my money in Saint Petersburg at an official exchange, a character came up to me and said he could give me a much better rate. The rate he was quoting me was definitely better than what they were charging at the official exchange. So I agreed to exchange with him instead. I got out my money, and he got out his. We were ready to make the deal. Then all of a sudden we heard police whistles blowing. The man panicked, and said that I had to take the money right away and run, or we'd both get arrested. So we quickly exchanged our paper money.

Maybe you can guess what happened next. The man quickly vanished with my money—and no cops showed up. It was a scam, plain and simple. The "cop" blowing the whistle was a friend of his, and the con man used the confusion to give me only half what my dollars were worth.

It took me twenty minutes just to get my breath back—and a little longer than that to admit to my family that I'd got scammed. I knew it was my fault; the crook offered me a deal, and I let him emotionally manipulate me. First, I let him make me feel savvy and excited about getting around the system; then I let him make me feel scared, and I didn't pay as much attention to the details of the deal as I should have. That's why you have to take emotions out of it when you're buying—because they'll cloud your judgment.

By the way, my family has never let me forget that bad deal!

The Worst You Can Hear Is "No"

I know negotiation isn't easy, especially as a buyer. Most people aren't used to haggling over prices on a daily basis. If you walk into the grocery store and see the milk priced at two dollars, that's what you're going to pay. The price of milk is the price of milk. But you shouldn't be afraid to ask for a lower price. The worst you can hear is "No." Most people don't negotiate at all, even when haggling is expected—like at a car dealership, for example. They build a cushion into the first price they quote you, same as I do. So as a buyer, if you take the step of asking for a better price, you're already ahead of a lot of other people.

Here's one simple thing to try if you're nervous about negotiating: If a price seems high to you, ask if the item is likely to go on sale anytime soon. If the answer is yes, follow up by asking if you can get the sale price now. If you can't get that discounted price now, you can always come back when the item goes on sale officially. But try it and see what happens. Asking for a lowered price and hearing "No" is good practice, too, even if you don't get any further than that.

Even big stores are now being set up to allow you to bargain a bit. Target offers price matching: If you can find a lower price online than what they're asking in their store, they'll match it. There are a few lines of fine print, but it's a genuine guarantee. They're sick of people using their store as a showcase to see the color of an item before buying it on Amazon. But you can be sure that most people, even if they've heard about this price-matching guarantee, are probably still too nervous to walk up to a salesperson in a Target and ask, "Can I get this toaster for five dollars off?" That's because most people just don't have any experience negotiating. But think about it—you know you're going to win this one. If you don't ask for the lower price, your fear just cost you five dollars. Even if you go home and buy that toaster on Amazon later, your fear cost you whatever you spent on gas to go to the store and not buy the item. Just ask.

If you want really good practice and examples of negotiation, go into a pawnshop. You can listen to people haggle for a little while before you try it yourself. Most of my customers know how to negotiate. I'd say about 80 percent of them have some experience haggling—they've been in pawnbrokers' shops before! We're ready for hagglers. You won't find a better place to practice your negotiation skills than a pawnshop. Just remember, the worst thing you can hear is "No"—and if you don't ask, the answer is a no anyway. So you might as well ask.

[CHAPTER 6]

Create Long-Term Success

I've been running my own business since I was thirty-one, and learning my trade since I was seven years old. I've learned a lot about how to build a business from the ground up, how to analyze the competitive landscape to come up with a unique but workable idea, how to minimize risks, and how to build a team that's committed to my vision. I've also learned how difficult it is to do all of this. In this chapter, I'll explain how important it is to

+ **know what problem your business is solving;**
+ **have a riskproof attitude;**
+ **hire partners, not employees; and**
+ **be ready to pay the price of entrepreneurship.**

My First Business Venture

In Oak Park in 1962, you couldn't buy pizza by the slice. How was I supposed to get through Hebrew school twice a week after school from 6:00 p.m. to 8:00 p.m., right in the middle of a suburban twelve-year-old's dinnertime, without anything to eat? I wanted to grab some pizza before class started, but at the time, I was a big kid: I wore a 36 husky, so I didn't need to eat the whole pizza by myself.

Well, luckily, the one time I caved and bought a whole pizza, I got swarmed by other kids from Hebrew school who all wanted a slice, too. I guess for some kids this might have been an opportunity to become the most popular guy in school. But for me it was an opportunity to make some money. I realized that first day that I wasn't the only kid who craved a slice of pizza before class started. I realized there was some pent-up demand there that I could profit from.

So I started buying a whole pizza twice a week and selling it for fifty cents a slice. Business was great. I got my pizza paid for, and then some. Pretty soon, business was so good I was able to expand. I knew I couldn't run a bigger business alone, so I brought my neighbor Dennis in as a partner, and we bought two pizzas a week. Then I decided to add a new product line—ice cream. Again, I knew expansion would require more manpower, so I brought in another kid. We'd clean out all the ice cream sandwiches we could get for a dime each, and we'd sell them for fifteen cents.

It was a limited-time-only sale: Get them before they melt!

Even the day the pizza was delivered late, I still made some money. The principal of the Hebrew school had seen me hustling every day. He'd come to appreciate my work ethic. So he kept the pizza in his office until after class—when I sold it for twenty-five cents a slice.

I made twenty dollars a week selling pizza and ice cream. For a twelve-year-old kid in 1962, that was a lot of money. Now, all these years later, the cash may be long gone, but the experience is still paying dividends.

Selling those pizzas was my first experience in building a business. Although I had been hanging around Popsie's pawnshop for a few years, this was the very first time I had built something of my own. My pizza empire might have been small, but I created it from scratch. I saw an opportunity, started selling on the ground to build a customer base, and expanded however I could. That's basically the same process I've followed in building my business at American Jewelry and Loan.

Know What Problem You're Solving

Like many great businesses, my pizza empire started with a desire to solve a problem I had experienced myself. Once I had the basic idea, I moved on to figuring out the mechanics of marketing and setting a price and, eventually, hiring employees. When you're creating a new business, you have to start by understanding your industry inside and out. What's the core demand? What will it take to break even? Where are your opportunities to expand? How will you set yourself apart from the competition?

With my pizza enterprise, the core demand was pretty obvious: Hungry kids wanted a slice of pizza. For a pawnshop, the core demand is for cash. Anyone who needs a quick, confidential loan can come to us as long as they have something of at least a little value to pawn. The item you're pawning serves as collateral for the loan. As long as you keep up with the interest payments, it's still yours.

It's in my best interest as the pawnbroker to have you pay me that interest, that steady stream of cash, rather than have you fall behind because then I have to take on the risk of selling your item when you can't redeem it. The best way for me to make money as a pawnbroker is to offer you a lower price in terms of the amount of the loan I'm willing to give you—not because I'm trying to cheat you, but because I don't want to set you up to fail.

I want you to be able to get your item back. That's why, for example, if you come in with a laptop worth $600, I might give you a $120 loan. If you don't redeem your item after a certain amount of time, it's mine to sell. An item like a laptop might not be worth very much if it's been in the warehouse for a year and there's a newer model out, but on the other hand, I've already made back some of the money I lent you through the interest you've paid me.

That kind of trade-off between pleasing the customer and protecting your bottom line can be tricky, but it's so important to get it right. Sure, some people are angry with me when I offer them a loan they think is less than what their item is worth. But I've been in business long enough that I know what my customer needs better than he does. He might think he wants a $500 loan on that $600 laptop, but I know he won't be able to pay it off. He'll be paying me interest for a while before eventually falling behind in his payments. In the end he'll have paid me for the privilege of taking his laptop off his hands and he won't be back to pawn with me again. I know that lower loan is ultimately better for both of us.

Whatever kind of operation you're trying to build, you have to start by knowing what problem your business is solving. For a pawnshop, the problem is simple: My customer needs cash and she doesn't have it. Staying focused on that problem helps guide me. I know loans are the core of my business, so I know I can compromise in other areas as long as I'm still making loans. The same is true for any business: Change what you have to and compromise in your adjacencies as long as you're still solving that core problem.

Know Your Business Inside and Out

You've also got to know your business inside and out in order to figure out how to strike a balance between pleasing the customer and giving away the store. When I'm making loans, I know I don't have to worry too much about what I could get for the item if I had to sell it. I can focus on a loan that's going to help out the customer and also be reasonably repayable and proportional to the value of the thing. People who sell something straight out are really only about 5 percent of our business, but we can give them a little more for their items because we can resell them after a two-week police hold so there's virtually no risk that the item will lose its value while sitting in the warehouse.

Especially when you start out, you need to do what's going to make your business different from the competition. You can't reinvent the wheel, but you can come up with an idea that's different enough that it'll set you apart. For me, that meant setting up shop in the nicer neighborhood of Oak Park. Most pawnshops are located in the seediest parts of town. My father didn't understand why we would want to move to a more affluent area, but I knew it would be the first step toward becoming a different kind of pawnshop, a place that would attract a different kind of customer and eventually change the image of pawnshops altogether. I knew my industry well enough to know what would work to make me different—and therefore more successful—than the other players.

As much as you want to set yourself apart from the competition, however, you don't want to spend every waking hour thinking about what others are doing. When I first started American Jewelry and Loan, I was absolutely the smallest pawnshop in Detroit. There was nobody, but nobody, making fewer loans than me.

I took out Yellow Pages ads in those days—as big as I could afford, which was only half an inch. My ads were tiny compared to my competitors' when I started out, but I tried not to pay any attention to the other guys' ads. I would have felt diminished if I did, so instead, I just paid attention to making my business bigger as fast as I could, and then the bigger ads would follow. I focused on growing and didn't pay too much attention to the Joneses. I don't want to keep up with the other pawnshops; I want to be the one everyone else is keeping up with.

Knowing your business inside and out means understanding both the big picture—the problem you're trying to solve—and the details. If you run a deli, you've got to know how long your customer will be willing to wait for her food, how many people in your neighborhood have dietary restrictions, how many people you're likely to have waiting at one time, and how you're going to lay out your shop so they're not stepping all over one another. You have to understand your customer's experience. Make it easy for people to do business with you. If you have a physical store, make it welcoming: clean, brightly lit, friendly, fun. Don't waste money you don't have on a fancy design, but do make sure you're not putting up any barriers that will keep people from walking in.

The same principle applies if your business is your own career: The more you know about your customer's needs, new trends in your industry, services your competitors are offering, and so on, the more valuable you'll be to your employer. Make it easy for your boss to do business with you: Take the time to read up on your industry, attend conferences to network and keep up to date on your field, take classes to keep your skills fresh, and show up to staff and one-on-one meetings with new ideas for how you, from your position, can help improve the end customer's experience.

Remember Louie from Sam's Loan? Before he came to work for my Popsie, he used to run a SuperStation, and he had a colorful way of describing what experience had taught him: "You gotta wipe the shit off the door handle if you want people to walk in." That may not be the nicest way to say it, but the principle is the same. Create a welcoming environment. Don't let anything keep your customer from walking in and giving you money. Even if your business is online, for your Web site, Facebook page, app, what have you, this principle still applies. And if you are your business, make sure you're maintaining a professional appearance and demeanor. Take a minute before you walk in the door every morning to collect yourself, so you're not bringing your stressful morning into work with you. Make it easy for your boss, your colleagues, and your customers to do business with you.

Know your business inside and out. Know what happens when the customer walks in your door. Know what your competitors are doing and what you're going to do differently. And most important, know what problem your business is solving. Everything else you're doing is in service to solving that problem.

· · ·

Riskproof Attitude

I designed my store to anticipate thieves. We have hundreds of televisions and thousands of laptops in inventory, but in terms of cash value, jewelry is 90 percent of our business. Some of it's in the vault, but we also have a lot of expensive merchandise out in our display cases every day. I designed the store so the good gold and diamond jewelry is all the way at the back, farthest from the door if somebody's trying to run out with it.

Theft is a constant problem in any retail business, including mine. We've got fifty thousand square feet crammed full of valuable merchandise—literally enough stuff to fill the bowling alley that my store used to be. I do my best to anticipate that risk and defend against it, and when we do get hit, if the theft exposed a weakness, I'll fix it. For example, when I first got a license to sell electronics as well as jewelry, I wanted to make sure my new merchandise was on display for the customer coming in off the street. I brought in my own stereo from home and put it in the window. The first time I left it there overnight, somebody smashed the window and took it. After that, you can bet I didn't leave merchandise in the window overnight anymore.

But no matter how much you prepare, you can't erase risk entirely. A few years ago, two crooks somehow got up on the roof of the store overnight. They spent hours cutting through the roof and then lowered one of the two down from the ceiling, *Mission Impossible*–style, and stole three fur coats. They were up on the roof for hours, in a snowstorm no less, but in and out of the actual store in less than a minute. There was no way I could have planned for that. We typically sell a full-length fur for about $100, and believe me, the damage to the roof cost a lot more than $300 to repair. I would have gladly given them the coats to avoid that bill.

In business, whether it's thieves or customers or competitors, people are always going to try to pull one over on you. The best you can do is think through the risks you can imagine and prepare for them as best you can by putting the jewelry way at the back of the store or taking a customer's sob story with a grain of salt. You also need to accept that despite your best efforts, you'll never be able to prepare for absolutely everything.

Sometimes you hit an obstacle you can't get past. Starting when I was twelve, I sold golf clubs out of my parents' basement. I started soon after I finished up with Hebrew school and my pizza-by-the-slice business came to its end. My dad pushed me to make some more money, and I was still saving up to buy that car, so he and Popsie let me try to sell some of the golf clubs we had in the shop. We had a lot of them, for whatever reason. I guess it's one of the first items people pawn if they need cash. In any case, I built a whole display in the basement and placed an ad in the paper to run on Saturdays. I'd be open for business on Sundays, when the pawnshop was closed. My ad would say "Dealer going out of business"—every week.

Business went really well for a while. The first day I was open, I made $40. I walked down to Hudson's, the department store, and bought myself two velour shirts for $4.99 each. Buying stuff with my own money made me feel like a young man instead of a little boy. I sold golf clubs for four years, and I made some good progress toward earning the money for the 1965 Mustang I wanted.

But then I ran into that obstacle I couldn't get past. One fateful day about four years into the business, two gentlemen in suits came in to look over my merchandise. They seemed like serious buyers. They took their time looking everything over and then they asked if they could come back after school on Monday to buy what they wanted. Well, they came back on Monday and showed me their badges: They were tax collectors for the state of Michigan. They were busting me for not charging sales tax.

They said I had two options: Fill out a bunch of forms and start charging the tax, or shut down. Obviously, I hadn't meant to do anything wrong. I was just a kid trying to earn a little extra money. But this issue was definitely one of those obstacles that I wasn't going to get past. I was still in high school, and I couldn't handle doing all that paperwork. I knew my side project was through. "Thanks very much," I told the tax collectors, doing my best to be polite despite my frustration. "This was my last day in business." I closed up shop for good, and soon after my golf "store" closed, I went into business making those chains and selling them to boutiques and then department stores.

Your business will never be riskproof, but your attitude can be. If you can't get through or past an obstacle, you've got to go around. If you can't do business the way you've been doing it, you've got to find a new way. There will always be obstacles. If you hit a cinder-block wall, you can either bash your head against it, or you can figure out a way around it.

When the economy was going down fast in 2008, it was hard to move our jewelry. Nobody had thousands of dollars to spend on a big diamond bracelet. Instead, we started making and selling small diamond stud earrings for $50. None of our customers had much money at that point, but people still wanted something bright in their lives. And it was a good way to take the larger pieces of jewelry that weren't selling and turn them into something that would bring in some cash. We sold hundreds of $50 earrings. Then a year or two later, when the novelty of those cheap earrings wore off for our customers, we ran a promotion that said if you bought gold jewelry, you would get the diamond for free. The downturn in the economy was a cinder-block wall I wasn't going to be able to bash my way through. I couldn't solve the whole economic problem on my own, but I could continue to move my merchandise and make money, so I figured out a way around it. My business wasn't riskproof, but my attitude was. Having a riskproof attitude means anticipating as much as you can and then being ready to roll with the things you didn't anticipate.

Who's Making Your First Impression?

Employees can add risk to your business, too. You can pour all your time and all your passion into your business, but if your employees aren't making an effort, it's not going to matter. You won't be the first person to greet everybody who walks through your doors. You've got to pay attention to the people who are forming your customer's first impression of your business. If you don't own your own business, this is even truer for you—your colleagues' behavior can influence the way clients and customers see you. Ever since the economy started to slide, I've been pushing customer service with all my employees. There are a lot of pawnshops in Detroit, but customer service isn't traditionally one of their strong points. For most of history, I think, pawnbrokers have taken the attitude that the customer is never right.

I figured that excellent customer service was one way I could set myself apart from my competition. After all, the only way to be seen as different from the rest is to actually be different from them. I told my employees they were to greet every customer with a smile. If somebody left our store without making a deal, I wanted my employees to say "I hope we can do better for you next time."

I tell my employees that this attitude applies to every person who walks through our doors. If they didn't think it was worth their time, they would be out of a job. It's simple stuff, but it does set us apart. I believe it helps make our customers more loyal. Generally, when people are coming into a pawnshop, they're already having a bad day. They need cash and they need it fast; that's stressful, to say the least. Anything we can do to make that situation easier on them, we try to do it.

You need to set a tone where employees aren't just polite and welcoming to customers but also to one another. Whether you're the boss or not, this starts with the way you treat the people around you. Our employee lunchroom can get pretty messy sometimes because, I guess, everybody thinks somebody else is going to clean it up. Whoever does take the time to clean up that place brightens everybody's mood and makes it a little easier for employees to focus on doing their jobs.

If employees are treating one another rudely or are fighting, they can't pay attention to customers in the way they should. Their attention is focused elsewhere, and it's a drain on their enthusiasm and energy. I remember in mid-2012, I started to get a lot of customer complaints about the service in my second store in Pontiac. People were having a hard time getting anyone to wait on them, and when they did get service, the clerks were disrespectful. The woman I had managing the place for me had worked her way up through the ranks for about twelve years. I trusted her. But I knew something wasn't right. So I had a talk with her and learned that her son was having problems at school. I said she could take a couple of weeks off to deal with the situation, but she needed to come back ready to set a better tone in the store. In the end she never came back; she couldn't get her head back in the game. It's always sad to lose a longtime employee, but in this case she had let her personal problems sour the whole shop's atmosphere. She hadn't dealt personally with tricky deals and prickly customers—she'd pushed that work onto somebody else's plate. That person resented doing extra work, and pretty soon the morale of all the employees suffered, and customer service started to suffer, too.

As a manager, the whole team's morale is your responsibility. That means you have to watch out for problems like this and take care of them as quickly as possible. As a team member, you can only control your own behavior—but you should remember that your behavior affects your colleagues. If you snap at your co-worker, he may turn around and snap at a customer, and that hurts the whole team.

Hire Partners, Not Employees

If your employees aren't up to snuff, it's going to be the downfall of your business. As easy as it is to become complacent in how you view your business and settle for the status quo instead of continually pushing to expand, it's also easy to start settling for less in terms of employee performance. But if you want your business to keep expanding, you've got to keep pushing your employees to do better.

The problem is that you can't force an employee to care about the business the way you do. Now, if you're an employee yourself, you can set yourself apart by taking pride in what you're doing and thinking of yourself as truly part of a team instead of just focusing on your own paycheck. But if you're managing employees, how do you get them to put in the effort you need?

My father had one strategy for getting his employees to work hard and listen to him. It wasn't all that different from his child-rearing strategy, to be honest. He was very rough with the employees: berating them, shouting, even getting physical with them. He broke his hand once when he hit one of our workers. I can't remember what the guy had done—it couldn't have been anything worth beating him up for. He broke another employee's arm once—I'm not even sure why. He basically thought that the Sam's Loan employees were beneath him, and he wasn't shy about showing it. You can bet we dealt with a lot of employee turnover in those days.

I've tried to take a different approach. My years running my own store have taught me that a world-class business doesn't need employees so much as partners—people who put their whole hearts into their work, just like I do. You can't beat that into people. Instead, you need to hire and train people to succeed in a system that encourages dedicated work.

In early 2012, I was having some trouble with the employees in the back room at the shop. There are about fifteen guys who work back there; they have a lot of inventory to move around, including plenty of electronics, and merchandise was getting broken. Now, I could have just threatened to fire them. That's certainly what my dad would have done. Instead, I bought them lunch. We sat down together and I told them that I understand accidents happen. "We're all in this together," I said. "We're partners. Just tell me if something breaks. Tell me why you think it happened and what you think we could have done differently. Help me figure out how we can prevent this. I need you to be my partners in solving this problem."

I try to see my employees as partners and I know that the attitude that we're all equals needs to start with me. I will never ask any of my employees to do something I wouldn't be willing to do—and there's very little I won't do or haven't done. Since I started running the store on my own, with just a few employees, I've done just about everything. I used to wash the windows in the store every morning. Still today, if I see something that needs doing around the store, I'll do it. I'll clean the toilets if they need cleaning. I believe that you can't expect an employee to do something correctly, with enthusiasm, if you won't do it yourself.

Showing your employees that you care about them as people will go a long way toward getting them to care about the business. I do my best to tell everyone who works for me that they're doing a good job—every day. In a way, it's like having fifty children. They're not perfect, they screw up, but part of the reason I get up every morning and go to work is to make my business better to provide for them and help them be successful as well. I couldn't have made it entirely on my own and I want the best for our shop and everyone who works with me.

One way to establish the feeling of partnership is making some kind of connection with everyone who works with you. There's one woman at the shop now who's studying to be a nurse. Sometimes I'll quiz her on the lists of drugs she has to memorize. When an employee came to me in tears because she'd just found out her father has cancer, I told her she could take the time off that she needed to care for him and her job would be safe. I know family is important to me, and if I want my employees to act like partners in my business, I have to treat them the way I'd want to be treated.

As soon as your business expands beyond what you can do yourself—as soon as you hire only your neighbor Dennis to help you sell slices of pizza—you're relying on employees to carry out your vision. They're the ones who form your customers' first impression of your business. They're making decisions every day that affect the way customers, suppliers, and community members see you. You need to hire partners, not employees, because you need your employees to care about your business.

Be a Partner, Not an Employee

I don't expect perfection from my employees. As long as they're doing their jobs correctly most of the time, as long as they're showing me a desire to succeed and that they care about the business, they don't need to close every deal or meet every goal. They can, and do, call me in for help if they're unsure about the right price to set, or they're dealing with a tricky negotiation.

That's not to say that their jobs aren't difficult. I have my fears to deal with, and I face them every day, but they have fears to face, too. When you work for somebody else, you may have to face the fear of losing your job unexpectedly, and that's a serious fear. Working under those conditions isn't for everybody.

I know that not everybody has the opportunity to build his own business. Maybe you don't have employees; maybe you work for somebody else. But whatever business you're in, even if it's the business of building your own career, the key to creating long-term success is to work hard and constantly look for the next opportunity to grow. If you are an employee, take the time to learn as much as you can about the business. If you work at a gym, for example, keep track of which classes, trainers, and promotions bring in the most new and repeat customers and figure out what you can do to support those initiatives. Show your boss that you care not just about your paycheck but about the health of the business. Clean up the lunchroom. Bring in candies or healthy snacks for the receptionist's desk. Volunteer to research the impact of a new regulation. Organize a community service project that will strengthen your office's connection to your community. Act like a partner, not just an employee. As an employer myself, I promise you, that's what your boss wants to see.

Paying the Price

If you're scared of work, you're never going to be successful. It sounds simple, but I've met a lot of people who want the victory without the fight. I've talked to friends who say they want to start a business, and maybe they even have some money saved up to get it started, but they haven't really thought through how much time they'll be able to devote to it, how big their potential market might be, or how much they can expect to make in the first year. People think they can build a business on enthusiasm and a cool new idea, but it takes a lot more than that. The hard truth is that successful people don't sleep much.

I love hard work—both in and out of the shop. I get up early every morning and work out because I believe it gets me ready for the day. I spend all day, every day, completely focused on growing my business. Spend a day with me and you'll see me answering questions constantly: My employees are always walking in to ask how much they can offer for this item or that and a million other questions.

I make a thousand decisions every day. Luckily, being a pawnbroker has taught me to think on my feet and make decisions quickly.

But there's a cost to all those decisions I make, day in and day out. When I get home and my wife asks me what I want to eat for dinner or what I want to watch on TV, I just don't care. I'm so invested in my business that I just can't make any more decisions after the workday is done and I'm off the clock for a few short hours. That's one of the reasons I wear pretty much the same outfit—jeans and a V-necked sweater—every day. I don't want to waste valuable time or brain power thinking about what to wear when I can be focused on my business instead.

It's hard for me to relax. Even in the car on the way home from work, I'm still making calls, making deals. I'm lucky if I get half an hour of downtime in a day. On occasion, I do go on vacation to the beach—and I try to relax, sometimes successfully. I'll take some time to just sit and smoke a cigar and look at the ocean, maybe listen to an audiobook. I spend so much time making decisions, it's a rare and great pleasure to take any time away from being "on."

If you want to run your own business, you have to get to know your industry, figure out what's going to set you apart from the competition, learn how to inspire your employees to care about your business—the list of tasks to complete, decisions to make, and skills to master never ends. That's the price of entrepreneurship. Running your own business takes a lot out of you. For me, it takes just about everything I've got.

That's part of the price of my success and I believe it's a price worth paying. Working this hard keeps me sharp. I'm sixty-two years old, and I know I'm not going to live forever, but I know I'll be working and thinking and striving until my time comes, whenever that is.

CHAPTER 7

Build Trust Throughout Your Community

Your reputation is all you have. Your business will live or die by it. You create your reputation every day, in every decision you make and every conversation you have. As a pawnbroker, I always start out with a couple of strikes against me. People assume pawnbrokers are shady characters. That's not true, but a few bad apples have soured the whole pawnbroking barrel. People assume my store is full of stolen goods or that I'm taking advantage of my customers. I've fought those accusations for years, and I've now built a reputation I can be proud of. In this chapter I'll tell you how I've built trust throughout my community by following these few simple rules:

+ **Deserve trust every day.**
+ **Don't listen to greed.**
+ **Believe that the good guys win.**
+ **Focus on relationships.**

Trust Starts with Transparency

A few years after I opened American Jewelry and Loan, I was working at the store one morning and noticed two men sitting in an unmarked car in the parking lot. A couple of hours later they were still there. Now, it was the middle of winter and I knew this shopping center, and I knew you don't usually see men sitting there in their cars all day.

There was only one possible explanation: They were from the FBI. They were keeping tabs on the store; pawnshops don't have the best reputation, and I was still pretty new in the neighborhood.

After a few hours, I walked outside and right up to the car. I knocked on their window and said, "Would you gentlemen prefer to sit inside? I can give you some hot coffee, and you can see what's going on a lot better inside than you can from out here." I wanted to make it easy for them, and I wanted to establish good relations with law enforcement. I knew I was running a clean business; I just needed to convince them.

They actually did come into the store that day. And they liked what they saw—no shady dealings. Those agents have since retired and live in Florida. We have been close friends for twenty-six years.

When you think of a pawnshop, I'm sure you think of a questionable business in a bad neighborhood whose only purpose is to provide quick cash to desperate people. Mostly, the business is really aboveboard today. There are procedures pawnbrokers have to follow to make sure we're not taking in stolen goods. We check IDs, and we take a thumbprint of everyone who pawns anything. The bottom half of every pawn ticket goes straight to the police department, with information on what has been pawned and who pawned it.

There are still some pawnbrokers who don't want the authorities to get that close to their business. Some jewelry buyers will still purchase a Rolex from somebody without fingerprinting or change the serial numbers on the merchandise they take in. It's a business where you're constantly walking a tightrope. It's very easy to fall and find yourself on the wrong side of the law.

The reality is that a secondhand dealer is a great place for a thief to get some quick cash for stolen goods if the dealer is willing to look the other way. Of course, if you do that, if you don't follow procedure, you're complicit in receiving stolen goods and the government can take away your license. As long as you do follow the procedure, you will not be prosecuted if somebody's pawned something stolen. You might even get reimbursed for whatever you paid for the item. For me, it's not worth it to take chances. Why would I jeopardize everything I've built? My practice has always been to be legitimate. Most pawnbrokers feel—and act—the same way. They do the best they can in an industry that is far more heavily regulated than in the past.

OK, so they don't give out medals for not breaking the law. But I've gone beyond just following procedure because to me, running a legitimate business is about more than just not getting caught doing something illegal. It's about my reputation in the community and the legacy I'm building for my kids. Transparency builds trust more than just following standard procedure.

That's why I didn't leave those agents in the parking lot. And that's why I've always approached the police as partners. I met with the police before I even made a deal with the landlord when I opened American Jewelry and Loan in its first location. I only needed a license, not necessarily their approval, but I wanted them to accept me and trust me. I wanted this store to be welcomed in the community, starting with law enforcement. Building trust is part of building a successful business that's not only going to make money, but will also build a legacy for that business—and for you. In order to build trust you have to deserve that trust every day, starting from day one.

Deserve Trust Every Day

In my early days at American Jewelry and Loan, when the business wasn't computerized and things weren't as easy to track, the pawn business had a reputation for being crooked. I didn't realize it at the time, but when I was applying for my license for the new store, the police were checking me out while the application was pending. The Oak Park Police Department would send in underage kids or undercover cops to try to catch me doing something underhanded. I thought that because I'd taken the initiative to talk to them up front about my plans for the store we were becoming friendly, but I now see that they were still testing me. They weren't going to trust me until I had proven myself to them, and the only way to do that was to steadily not disappoint them.

Most pawnbrokers would never bring the authorities into their store, so that first move set me apart. But trust, like Rome, can't be built in a day. If I truly want the cops to see me as a partner, I have to treat them with respect and operate transparently every single day I'm in business. When something comes into my store that rings warning bells in my head, such as an offering of gold I think might be stolen, I don't wait for the cops to come in with a search warrant; I call them to let them know about a suspicious item someone just brought in. My goal is not just to cooperate—I don't want stolen merchandise in my store at all if I can prevent it.

Of course, sometimes I get beat. People sneak things past me. Recently a man came in with a four-carat square diamond, set with some smaller diamonds in the band. It was a lovely piece of jewelry and we lent him $5,500 against it. But unbeknownst to me, the state police in western Michigan were looking for this ring; it had been stolen in a home invasion. They ended up busting this thug, a drug dealer, for the home invasion, and in his house they found a pawn ticket and piles and piles of $5 bills, which he claimed was the cash he got for legitimately pawning his own item. Well, you can see where this is going. That pawn ticket was from my store.

I didn't wait for the police to get a search warrant; I turned in the ring to them right away.

I would rather help them out before they ask for help if I can. And I get kind of a kick out of it. I let the police do the police work, but if I can help catch some bad guys, I won't say no. I treat the cops like partners every single day because the only way to make them trust me is to deserve their trust.

· · ·

Be a Good Partner

Sometimes being careful about stolen goods means passing on a really great deal. A customer once came into my store with a box full of gold rings. The rings would weigh about ten pounds melted down, and the man wanted $20,000 for them. My eyeballs almost popped out of my head. That much gold would be worth $120,000. That was a potential $100,000 profit. That was huge—and it was early in my ownership of the store, too, when I really needed the cash.

But something was off. I could smell mildew in the box, and the rings still had price tags on them. I was pretty sure that this character had ripped off a jewelry store, buried the rings, gone to jail for six or seven years, and then got out, dug up the box, and walked into my store to sell them for quick cash. While the customer waited out front, I took the tag from one of the rings, went into the back of the store, and called up one of my friends at the FBI and another friend who was a chief of police. I asked them to look up these rings in their systems and see if they were flagged as stolen goods.

Neither of my friends called me back right away, so I had to tell the customer I couldn't buy his gold. I didn't feel I could take a risk on gold I thought was stolen. You know I hate letting money walk out the door, but I was pretty certain that merchandise was hot. I didn't want to blow it entirely because of the small chance it was legiti-mate, so I told the man to come back to the store the next day. Maybe, just maybe, I'd have a better answer.

Finally, my friends in law enforcement called me back at the end of the day. The rings weren't in the system. Both friends advised me to buy the gold; as far as they were concerned, it was all aboveboard. "I sure hope you bought that stuff," my FBI friend actually said. I couldn't believe it. "Son of a bitch, I let it go," I replied.

Of course, it was too late for that $100,000 I was hoping to make. Luckily, the customer did come back to the store the next day and although he had sold most of the merchandise to other places, I was still able to buy about a quarter of it.

I hated losing that big deal. It was the kind of catch pawnbrokers dream about. In the end, though, I know I did the right thing by waiting and calling my friends to check the goods out. In the long run, it's very useful that I have genuinely good relationships with people whom a lot of pawnbrokers would see as the enemy. The cops and agents try to protect my interest, too, whenever they can. Twenty years ago, I bought three paintings from a customer for $5,000 total. They were pretty small, but I could tell they were quality work that could be sold in a reputable gallery. In fact, I liked the paintings so much I brought them home to Lili.

Well, that night when the eleven o'clock news came on, one of the top stories started out with "Robbery today at noted gallery..." They flashed pictures of the stolen paintings on the news. They were my paintings! I called my friend, the chief of police, and he helped me get the paintings back to the gallery. Even better, they made sure the gallery owner gave me a reward to help cover the cost of what I'd spent to buy the things.

Law enforcement looks out for me because over the years I've built good relationships with many of the officers and agents I've known. Our relationship has gone beyond their looking out for me; they now know I'm also looking out for them. One chief of police used to sometimes call me for business advice. He may run a public institution, but he still has employees and labor issues. Because he knows I run a good business, he can also trust me to give him good guidance on motivating employees, for example.

The police know I'll always try to help them out. As an example, there was a string of jewelry store robberies in town a while back. The police called to tell me they'd traced some of the material to another pawnshop in town, one of my competitors, but the owner wouldn't give the merchandise back. I knew the pawnbroker; his grandfather and my Popsie were in the business together. I gave him a call and said, "Listen, do you want to be a hero or do you want to be an asshole?" I talked him into giving the merchandise back, so the jewelry stores were made whole and the police were able to use it as evidence to trace the crooks and end the string of robberies.

I encourage other people in my industry to behave the way I do with respect to the police. I'm trying to be the best possible partner for my friends in law enforcement that I can be. And that means doing everything I can to deserve their trust every day.

Never Cut Corners

My dad didn't subscribe to the same belief I did when it came to running his business with trust and transparency—especially when it came to law enforcement and regulations. He got a grilling from the cops once because he transposed a serial number when writing a ticket for a shortwave radio. I don't know if it was a mistake in recording the numbers or if he was trying to get away with something shady, but he did get heat from law enforcement for that. Because potentially that's receiving and concealing. Even if it was a legitimate mistake, in the eyes of the authorities, he was receiving and concealing, violating procedure.

Even that incident didn't change my father's attitude about how to operate a pawnshop. He and I never saw eye to eye on the right way to do business: I was always a pretty straitlaced kid while he was always more willing to get involved in shadier deals. I don't think it helped that he'd been a pool hustler before he went into the pawnshop business. He'd learned early, and the wrong things. But I was way more reserved and on the level. Back in the sixties, when a lot of my friends were into drinking and doing drugs, there I was selling golf clubs out of my parents' basement and walking all over town trying to sell the gold chains I made. I wasn't the coolest kid, but I was the most focused.

I also remember that my dad, along with most of the other pawnbrokers in Detroit at that time, would give out little gifts to the cops around the holidays. I was never quite comfortable with that because it felt like bribery, but my father said it was the way business was done. Popsie may have given out gifts at Christmas, too, but I never saw him do it.

The first Christmas in Oak Park, I gave the local police lieutenant a holiday card with fifty dollars in it. I'd always been taught that was the thing to do! But as soon as he opened the card, he called me up and said, "You've got to get down to the station right away."

I thought, *Well, now I'm in trouble.* I got to the station and the officer pulled me into an interrogation room. "Look," he said, "we are friends, but you can't ever do anything like this again."

That was a good lesson for me. Not everything is quid pro quo; that doesn't build trust. The only thing you can do is deserve trust every day. Your reward will come eventually.

Greed Isn't Good

Greed is natural; it's human—but it's not good for business. All too often people in business will let greed get the better of them. A year ago, when we were filming one of our shows, a customer came in trying to sell a van owned by Dr. Death, Jack Kevorkian. The customer owned a car dealership and had bought the van four years earlier on eBay, and now he wanted to sell it. He had the title and the VIN: It all checked out. The man wanted six figures for the van. I was interested, but I wasn't *that* interested. I mean, I wanted to buy the van but only to donate it to the Henry Ford Museum. It was a piece of history; that's where it belonged.

The guy asked for $100 grand for the van and I came back with $20 grand. He said 70. I responded with 20. He went to 60. I said 30. Finally, I got him to come down to $35 grand, but I still couldn't quite decide whether the van was worth that price.

At this point, Ashley and Seth got involved. The customer looked like he was enjoying the action, so Ashley offered an idea she'd seen me use once or twice. She said, "Let's flip a coin. Heads, we'll give you forty thousand dollars; tails, we'll give you twenty thousand." The customer liked that idea. We got the coin, and I gave him one more chance to hedge his bet and get a better offer; I said he could flip the coin for either $25,000 or $35,000.

But I could see in his eyes that he was greedy and wouldn't take the better deal. He wanted to try for the $40,000.

He picked heads. The coin landed on tails. The look on his face was priceless, but the deal wasn't. I bought the van for $20,000.

Normally, when you make a big bet like that, your heart starts beating fast. I'll bet that customer was pretty worked up. But I was calm as can be because I knew I wasn't being greedy. If you're greedy, you're going to lose.

Greed is human and, unfortunately, so is dishonesty. Anytime we can justify a little bit of cheating to ourselves, we'll do it. I see that a lot in my shop. We get people walking into the store all the time who've conveniently forgotten that the thing they're about to pawn doesn't belong to them.

For example, quite a few people who get a computer from their workplace convince themselves it's theirs because they've been using it for a while, and then they bring the computer in to try to pawn it. But that is illegal, no matter how much that thing feels like it's yours. We end up doing a lot of recovery for Detroit Public Schools with merchandise like this. We had a customer come in with a laptop, and when my buyer took a closer look at it, he saw that there was a sticker on the bottom that claimed it was the property of some laboratory or other. As soon as my buyer pointed out that embarrassing fact, the customer ran right out of the store.

The bad news for business owners is that the more distance there is between the liar and the lie, the easier it is to justify. Often it doesn't even take much distance. Apparently, people don't believe they're cheating when they kick a golf ball into a better position instead of reaching down and picking it up with their hands. The distance between the brain and the feet may be all the distance needed. For most people it would be pretty tough to walk into my store and flat-out lie to me. But for a business owner, it might be pretty easy to, say, transpose some numbers on a form and then pretend it was an honest mistake.

The solution is to remind yourself of your commitment to honesty. Most people won't cheat on a test if there's a statement about an honor code written on the top of the answer sheet. Try putting something in your office that reminds you that you want to live with integrity, such as a picture of a respected family member or an award you won for good citizenship. Temptation is everywhere and you need to make sure you can't justify bending the rules. Seth gave me the old Sam's Loan sign for my sixtieth birthday that I have hanging in my office, but I didn't put it there to keep me honest. I put it there so I would think about Popsie every day. He reminds me that family comes first, and that I have to always build my business in ways that will make my family proud by keeping it clean and aboveboard. That's how I can make sure it's long term, too.

It's also easier for people to resist temptation when they're thinking about the future. If you're on a diet, it's easier to resist buying a box of cookies at the supermarket when you're planning your meals for the week than it is to resist buying a slice of pound cake at Starbucks when you're hungry at the moment. I try to always stay focused on the long term: the legacy I want to leave for my kids and grandkids and the relationships I want to build with the people in my community. That focus on the future helps me be less greedy.

Resisting temptation isn't only important for pawnbrokers or other folks working in an industry with a shady reputation. Any business has opportunities for greed to creep in. Any working career will bring moments when your integrity is tested. Make sure you pass those tests.

Integrity Will Set You Apart

Not all people operate with integrity. I learned that the hard way when I tried to go into business with a friend back in the late eighties after we were starting to make good money in our shop. He had the idea to open up a bar in Detroit with a retro fifties theme. Lili and I decided to take the risk and invest in the bar—and it was a huge success. We sold $1 million worth of liquor in the first year. Still, even though the bar was always packed and we should have been raking in money, I was having trouble making payments on the loan we'd taken out to make the investment. My partner said we were losing money. Then one day, about two years into the business, my sister-in-law took us out on her boat on the lake. We were having a nice time enjoying the evening until we spotted our business partner's girlfriend on a huge new boat nearby. We got suspicious because it was such a fancy, expensive boat. We investigated a little and found out that our business partner had added a $5 fee to get into the bar some nights. We hadn't seen a penny of all that extra money. The guy was a thief.

He must have wanted to get caught. Why else would he name the boat *Cover Charge*?

That was an educational experience for me. And I get more examples of such shady dealings every time I open the newspaper, whether it's Enron or the London Whale. Even when you go to the bank, you can't necessarily trust that they're giving you a fair and honest deal—look at what happened with mortgages a few years ago. Bankers got greedy and started offering mortgages to everyone, even people who couldn't afford them; then they sold the mortgages as investment vehicles and made tons of money until the whole house of cards came crashing down. Your business can't afford to make a similar mistake.

Those constantly occurring corporate scandals add up to a depressing state of affairs for the world, but they also create an opportunity. If you deal honestly with people and show them your word can be trusted, that's a huge advantage in a world where trust is in short supply. I believe part of my store's success comes from the fact that I deal honestly with everyone: customers, police, the government. Don't listen to greed—your integrity will set you apart.

Being Good Is Good for Business

Obviously, there's no guaranteed benefit to your bottom line when you build relationships with law enforcement. There's no automatic profit in being friends with the cops. But to me it's all part of running a business that's a welcome, trusted part of the community. In my line of work, sometimes that means helping the cops catch bad guys by turning in stolen merchandise with a description of the seller. For other businesses it might be reaching out to a local school or homeless shelter or community organization. Doing charity work can seem like a distraction when you're crunched for cash and you're just trying to keep your doors open day to day, but I know from experience that it is always worth your time to make that call.

My history with law enforcement has sometimes helped my business and sometimes cost me a penny or two. More important is the long-term perspective. Early in the 1980s, through my friendships with cops, I started to make some connections with politicians, including the state attorney general. The attorney general called on me for help when the price of gold went way up and the government wanted to strengthen the rules on secondhand gold buyers, adding more stringent registration requirements to make it harder for them to sell under the counter. Gold had gone up so quickly that people were selling it out on street corners, and there was a big uptick in home invasions, too. The state attorney had some ideas for changing the rules on how gold buying was reported to the state, and he came to me for advice about whether the changes were strong enough—could I see any way folks could get around the new rules?

I helped him out because we were friends, but that connection did help me later. Since 1917, the state law in Michigan has more or less stated that a pawnbroker has to hold an item in pawn for six months before selling it, and he can only charge 3 percent interest a month on the item. And when the pawnbroker sold it, he owed the balance of the proceeds above the interest back to the person who pawned the item initially. Most pawnbrokers would set up a legally separate company and sell the merchandise out of pawn at no profit, and then have the second company sell the item at retail to make their money.

I wanted to change that law. I decided the key was going to be changing the clause about the title; I wanted the pawnbroker to own the item if the customer didn't redeem it in time. There was no good from having my business rely on some legal loophole to own an item. I wanted the title fair and square.

In 1997, I got together with the former state attorney general (the friend I helped with the gold laws) and we started discussing changing that law. He gave me some good advice on how to navigate the legal process. Basically, it's like another kind of negotiation. We would go in asking for the right to charge 5 percent interest a month, up from 3 percent, plus a dollar-a-month storage fee, up from fifty cents, and the title to the item.

His tactics worked. Of course, as in any negotiation, we didn't get everything we asked for. The new law kept the interest at 3 percent a month, but it increased the storage fee to $1 a month. If you've got a thousand loans on your books, that's $1,000 a month in revenue. But more important, we got the point that mattered most—the title.

The former attorney general wouldn't have worked with me to lobby for those changes if I hadn't built a relationship with him. You can't go into a relationship expecting a quid pro quo; but a solid friendship will certainly never hurt your business, and you never know when a connection to the right person might help.

Also, I never would have gotten a TV show if I hadn't been running a legitimate business. Obviously, the episodes show the more colorful side of pawnbroking. You'll see people kicking up a fuss, getting thrown out of the store, and yelling at me. But you won't see me or my kids or my employees cutting any legal corners. We wouldn't have been able to build this partnership with the TV folks if we operated underhandedly the way some pawnshops do. In order to build a show around us, they had to know they could trust us. Being trustworthy can bring you opportunities. You've got to believe that the good guys will win in the end. That's certainly been my experience.

It's All About the Dash

My Popsie was a handshake kind of guy. You could count on his word, and customers could rely on him to give them a fair price. I've always tried to live up to his example. If I give my word to someone, I stick to that. If we set a price on a deal, and I find out later that the item's worth a lot more or less than I thought, I'm not going to try to renegotiate. I want to leave a legacy of trust just the way Popsie did.

A lot of people in the pawnbroking business don't want their kids to be in it. Me, I can't tell you how thrilled I am that my kids are working with me, because I've always known that pawnbroking doesn't have to be about under-the-table deals with criminals. It can be about helping families, helping your neighbors, and helping your community.

When you're down in the ground, six feet under, with two dates and a dash on your headstone, all that matters about your life is that dash. What did you do while you were here? What are people going to say about you when you're gone? I think about the implications of my legacy every day when I'm making decisions about my business.

Seth came up with an idea recently that would help build trust with new customers. He suggested that we offer any new customers loans at zero percent for the first month. Pretty soon a lot of other pawnbrokers jumped on our bandwagon, so now people in the area can bounce their items around from store to store for a while and avoid paying interest at all. But we're sticking with the offer because we believe it's a great way to introduce people to our store and build our customer base.

I always want to deal fairly with people and give them the benefit of the doubt whenever I can. Working in a pawnshop, you've got to be ready to hear some bullshit, but if customers aren't trying to cheat me outright, I will try to work with them. My father basically assumed the customer was always wrong. I don't think the customer is always right—you can't in a pawnshop—but I do think the customer is sometimes right. In my business, that attitude is pretty generous.

If a customer buys a television from me without a warranty, for example, I might still exchange the item for her if it breaks. For me, the bottom line is preserving the customer relationship. That's what's most important. A customer came in a while ago and bought a forty-two-inch TV. We helped him put the TV in his car. He came back the next day with it—cracked. Now, I knew he was the one who broke the item, but his brother works for me, and my relationship with my employee is worth more to me than the $400 the customer paid for the TV. I gave him his money back.

Your reputation is ultimately your most important possession. That's the legacy you're going to leave when you're gone. And if you focus on relationships every day, you'll end up leaving the legacy you want.

You're Here to Help People

I know it might not be the first thing you think of when you think of a pawnshop, but I really do try to help people if I can. I've found some really loyal customers with that approach. One of my best relationships is with Cora McCann. She has pawned with us more than six hundred times over thirty years. She has diabetes and needs daily medications. Her disability checks didn't always arrive on time and she needed cash to carry her over a few days so that she could pay for her medication. She would come in about every three weeks and pawn three TVs and a portable radio. We always gave her more money than the items were worth because we knew she needed us, and we knew we could help her out.

It sounds a little corny, but that's my higher purpose: helping people—helping my customers, helping my community, helping my family and my employees' families. Focusing on that gets me out of bed in the morning and keeps me working hard all day. And I think my employees work harder when they have that ideal in mind, too. Focusing on the reason your business exists will help you work harder, help you remember to do the right thing, and help you build a better business or be a better employee.

People know a lot more about businesses today than they used to, and they know especially that if you're building something new, one bad interaction, one customer or client who walks away feeling mistreated, can ruin your reputation. Every conversation matters. That's what I believe, and that's what I try to teach my employees. The only way to get a reputation for being trustworthy is to be trustworthy, and then keep being trustworthy, for thirty or forty years. Focus on relationships, remember that the good guys will win in the end, ignore the voice of greed, and make sure you deserve trust every single day. I believe I've done that at American Jewelry and Loan, and I believe it's one of the secrets of my success.

[CHAPTER 8]

Put Family First

I've told you about the challenges of running a business and the price I pay for devoting myself to my work. Now it's time to tell you what keeps me going. It takes a lot of energy to build a business, to chase a dream, or to change your life. Ultimately, the only thing that can keep you strong through all those struggles is love. Your family, whatever it looks like, needs to be your motivation because if you're only in it for yourself, you're not going to be strong enough to do all the work required to go above and beyond. In this chapter I'm going to talk about love

+ **as a source of strength in hard times;**
+ **as the foundation of a family business; and**
+ **as a fuel that will make any business stronger.**

Family First

After everything you've read about what my family was like when I was growing up, you may be wondering why in the world I'd advise anybody to put family first. Yes, when I was younger, aside from my grandparents, my family was dominated by my father, who was always putting me down and holding me back. Family meant fights and heartbreak. I did have Popsie and Bubbie as examples of what a close and loving family could be. But once they were gone, family in my life was a source of strife, not strength.

Until I met Lili.

Lili used to work in a women's clothing store that my cousin frequented. That cousin first tried to set us up when I was twenty and Lili was just sixteen; Lili told her to forget about it because I was too old for her. Lucky for me, my cousin tried to set us up again, four years later, and this time Lili agreed to give me a chance.

Our first date was hardly even a date. Lili came over to my house, and she and I and another one of my cousins sat around eating pistachios and talking. I told her early in the evening that my birthday was coming up, and if things went well, she could spend my birthday with me. She said, "Let's just see how the evening goes first."

That night, I drove her home around 1:30 in the morning and we sat in the driveway talking for another couple of hours. Around 3:30 her dad suddenly walked out of the house. I thought he was going to come straight to the car and kill me for keeping his daughter out so late, but he was just heading out to his job at a slaughterhouse. Lili just said, "Good morning, Daddy," as calm as could be. This was my first glimpse of the trusting, supportive family I was about to be welcomed into.

We'd had such a great time talking that night that I did take her out on my birthday, June 20. We went horseback riding and then I took her out for dinner. After that we saw each other every single day. There was never a day that we were not together. We both just knew that was it, right from the beginning.

After just a few dates, she said, "Listen, there are other guys calling me. If you're just going out with me to spend some time, I'm not interested. But if you're willing to make a commitment, I'm interested." She knew how to negotiate—and how could I say no to that offer? Clearly, I was interested.

We started going out in June, and in December, I said, "If I were to ask you to marry me, would you say yes?" She said she would, but it took me another year to work up the nerve to ask her for real. Even then, I never actually said the words "Will you marry me?" to Lili. I was too nervous. I just told her to reach into the back pocket of my jeans, where I had hidden the ring earlier in the day. When she pulled it out and saw it, she said, "Does this mean we're getting married?"

It may not have been the perfect proposal, but it worked! We got married the following year, in April 1976.

We started our life together at the same time I began to build a new business. When we got married, I was still working at Sam's Loan but starting to plan for the new store that would become American Jewelry and Loan. Ashley was born in 1978, the same year we opened American Jewelry and Loan. Money was tight for a while, as you can imagine. Little children meant big bills. Every dollar I took in that I didn't need for the family went back into building the business. Through all of that, Lili kept me grounded. She kept me focused. I'd come home stressed out, worried about paying the bills, and she'd look at me and tell me we were going to make it. Just hearing her say that to me was a huge help.

I had the business sense, but she gave me the emotional strength to get through those lean years.

Sure, we bickered a little every now and then. We still do. Of course it's usually my fault. But in reality, I'd do anything to make her happy. I'd even make a bad deal. We went to an art fair recently and saw some beautiful glass menorahs. Lili loved them, so I went to negotiate with the artist. The woman asked for $2,000 for three pieces. I offered her $1,500. She said no. So I walked away. I'm a pawnbroker. I'm always ready to walk away. As far as I'm concerned, there's always another deal about to walk in the door. But Lili wasn't happy. She wanted those menorahs. So I paid full price. I'd bend almost any of my own rules for the woman who's gotten me through the hardest times in my life.

Lili's family has also been a source of strength for me over the years. She and her parents and sisters were all very close. We had dinner with them every Thursday night for years. I needed their support and love as much as I needed Lili's. Building a business from scratch is incredibly challenging. It'll take just about every scrap of energy you have. But love can be a source of strength in those hard times. Lili and her family taught me that.

• • •

What Happens When You Put Business First

I needed another example of what a functional family could be like because those early years building American Jewelry and Loan were particularly bad ones for me and my parents. The older and more successful I got, the more my father resented me. I think he was threatened by me.

I now know that sometimes, when I wasn't around, he would tell his friends he was proud of me. He was impressed by my success, but he'd never say it to my face. And he'd never let that stop him from trying to cause trouble for me. My father used to say you screw your friends first—and, unfortunately, he put that motto into action.

He set the tone for our dysfunctional family, and it affected all of us. Even my sister and I went through periods where we didn't speak. It seemed like things were going to stay the same forever, but in the end he pushed all of us too far.

My mom had always suspected my father of cheating on her. I remember one night when the whole family went out to a casino party because at the time it was one of the few places where you could get good shrimp, and a woman came up to us out of nowhere and dumped a whole plate of spaghetti on my father's lap. Apparently, he'd said something inappropriate to her in the buffet line. Well, my mother finally had had enough. After years of fighting like two bulls, my parents finally got a divorce in 1980. It made a lot of sense in some ways, but of course it meant my mother would need her own source of income. I offered to support her out of the proceeds from American Jewelry and Loan. The store was only two years old, but I told her I could guarantee her $75,000 a year, plus all the jewelry she wanted. Meanwhile, I was counting on paying myself only $50,000 a year. It was going to be tough, but I was raised to take care of family, even to put family ahead of myself, and I was determined to take care of her.

The divorce was long and bitter, and my mother became depressed. She started to feel that everyone was against her. And somehow her lawyer managed to convince her that I was colluding with my father to keep part of the profits of our two stores from her. I got home one day and found a subpoena on my door. She'd closed my safe deposit boxes and was summoning me to testify in the divorce proceedings about this supposed conspiracy between my father and me.

That was one of the worst days of my life.

I couldn't understand how my mother could do that to me. She'd always been more supportive of me and was willing to say she was proud of me. And I had meant it when I offered to support her. I would have worked my butt off to keep her comfortable. She'd had an aneurysm about ten years before this incident, and every single night I'd go to her house and put my arm around her and walk with her to help her get her strength back. I was ready to put her needs first. I would never have screwed over anyone in my family, no matter what my father's attitude was.

That was one of the low points in my life, that falling-out with my mother. But, fortunately, we did reconcile several years later. Unbeknownst to me, after the kids were born she used to drive by our house hoping to catch a glimpse of them. One day Lili ran into her at a restaurant, and they got to talking. She told my mother she would help get us talking again. Lili set something up so we could talk. And by then, in 1986, she was in a better place and she understood that I'd been on her side during the divorce. So I got my mom back.

My father and I never had that kind of reconciliation. Our final falling-out started in 1981 when Seth was born. Despite everything he'd put me through, I wanted my father to be with me when my son was born. I guess I was still hoping we'd eventually have the kind of family Popsie had shown me was possible, the kind of family that Lili had and that she and I were starting to build. But he wouldn't leave the store, even to be there with me when my son was born. He said to me, "I only close for funerals."

That was the last straw for me. I knew then that we had no hope of building the kind of relationship I'd had with Popsie and that Lili had with her parents. I finally understood that family didn't matter to him. The only thing that mattered to him was the money he could make inside those four walls on Michigan Avenue. He was always a big spender—he liked to look successful, with a nice car and a wife wearing big jewels. He lived beyond his means just trying to show off.

When I went back to work a couple of weeks after Seth's birth, I sat down in my dad's office at Sam's Loan and confronted him about the business. We were supposed to be fifty-fifty partners in the store. Like a fool I had trusted that the paperwork would back up the verbal understanding that we had. And true to form, he had screwed me over. I asked him point-blank, "If a chain is worth ten dollars, how much of it is mine?" "I guess about two dollars," he replied.

Two dollars—20 percent. The paperwork didn't say I was a 50 percent partner; it said I owned 20 percent of the store. I should never have trusted his word.

So I walked out. Three years after opening American Jewelry and Loan, I bought him out of it, and I left my grandfather's store forever. My father believed I'd be back. He just had to try to put me down one last time, I guess. But I was sure I'd never return to working with a man who was supposed to love me—and treated me so poorly. And I never did.

After that argument, I went home to Lili. It was the middle of the day. She was standing in the laundry room holding Seth, who was two weeks old. She asked me what I was doing home, and I told her I'd quit working for my father. Right away she told me she knew we'd be fine. She always had such confidence in me. Like Popsie used to do, she helped me to keep believing in myself.

Lili kept me going through those first years building up the new business while I was dealing with all of this nonsense. She never stopped believing that I was going to be successful. That support was so important to me. I couldn't have built my business without it. Her love was a source of strength for me in those hard times. And she showed me that our family could be different from the mess I grew up with. From the very first day I walked into American Jewelry and Loan as its sole owner, I knew I wanted to be as different from my father as possible. And that meant always putting family first.

Working with the People You Love

Now I'm working with my own kids, and I'm even more aware of how important it is to put our relationships above our business. I tried to set the tone from the beginning that we're always going to be a family first and a family business second. My father didn't want me to call him Dad because it made him feel old. Well, the first day Seth came to work for me, I sat him down and I said, "You're my employee from 9:30 a.m. to 6:00 p.m.

every day, but from 6:05 p.m. to 9:25 a.m. you're my son. We're going to argue. Expect it. But at the end of every day, we'll kiss and make up because we're still family."

And he's always going to call me Dad.

It's easy for a family business to become a source of strife. It certainly was between me and my father. But I never want that to happen with my kids.

I don't mind if I see Ashley and Seth arguing about the business—that's bound to happen. If you watch our show, you know it happens all the time. We've all got strong personalities and we're passionate about what we do, so feelings can run high at times. But I have set the tone that those arguments end when we close up shop for the day. Those arguments don't affect us as a family.

And Seth and Ashley aren't always fighting; there are plenty of days when I get to see my two kids working together, making deals together, and getting along, and I just love that. It brings tears to my eyes.

Seeing them working together makes me feel like a success more than anything else that happens with the business. That's my dream now, to keep this business going for them and for their kids. I'd like to see American Jewelry and Loan all over the United States three generations from now. I'd like my great-grandchildren to be able to watch me on TV. That's my dream now.

I love watching my kids work and seeing the different strengths they bring to the business. They're very different people, but they've both got qualities the business needs. Ashley's more like me than Seth is: She wrote her first loan when she was seven and a half years old, not even tall enough to see over the counter. She used to come to work with me every Saturday when she was a kid, just like I did with my grandfather. We'd stop and get a McDonald's breakfast meal on the way in, and she'd help me write loans all day.

She's always had the same love of the business as I have. She understands the customer; she has the pawn-broker mentality; she gets that same kind of thrill that I do from making a deal.

Seth, on the other hand, really didn't take to the busi-ness when he was younger—and that's putting it mildly. Working at the pawnshop for him was a little bit like going to the dentist and getting a tooth pulled without novocaine.

I think it was hard for him because we lived in a nice neighborhood, and his friends' parents were doctors and lawyers, and there was his dad, the pawnbroker. He was naturally a conservative kid, and I'm pretty loud and outspoken—definitely different from all the other dads. Seth is very bright: always made the honor roll, got a 4.0, and graduated from the University of Michigan. His dream was to become a psychiatrist. He wanted to be like his friends' parents, I guess.

I always needed extra help at the store in December, the busiest time of the year for the retail side of the business. Even when she was a teenager, Ashley loved coming in to help out, but Seth used to make excuses to try to get out of coming in to work. It was always too cold or too snowy or he was too busy; there was always something keeping him away.

So I was truly surprised when sometime in his junior year at Michigan, Lili told me he'd called while we were away on vacation. I asked her what he'd said, and she said, "Oh, he says he wants to get into the business."

"What business is that?" I said.

Well, it was the family business, of course. He'd finally seen a place for himself at American Jewelry and Loan. He had decided to switch his major to business and come and work with me. I think that as he got older he started to better understand how hard I've worked and to see the value of what I've built at American Jewelry and Loan.

His place at the store was never going to be out on the floor. It took him a little while to settle into pawnbroking—a few years of just being there every day and seeing how things work. He doesn't have the same feel for pricing that I do, and being out on the floor doesn't come as easily to him as it does to me or Ashley. He's not a natural salesman—he's a little too shy for that.

But he's developed a great head for how to run a business, and he has a vision for where our business can go in the future. He's the one who's built up our online presence, and now we're drawing 15 percent of our revenue from online sales. And he's good at enforcing discipline on the staff, better than I am, really. I can be kind of a pushover sometimes.

Because of how Seth used to feel about pawnbroking, I really never expected to end up running a family business again. But I'm grateful to have that opportunity. When I first started American Jewelry and Loan, I was building it for my children. Now I'm building it *with* my children. And that makes everything I'm doing so much more meaningful.

Loving the People You Work With

Now that I am running a family business again, I'm thinking about what kind of business I'll be passing on, when the time comes, and whom I'll be passing it on to. I know it's a big challenge for a family business, transitioning to the next generation. A lot of times, when you leave a business to your kids, the kids screw it up. Apparently, only 10 percent of family businesses make it to the third generation.

But it is possible to make a family business last. There's a hotel in Japan, the Hoshi Hotel, that's been owned by the same family for forty-six generations. I'm confident that American Jewelry and Loan will be around for a fourth generation and beyond. Not just because I know my kids are smart, tough, and hardworking. I also know that they're a team, they both have different strengths, and they're surrounded by a group of co-workers whom I have handpicked to bring other necessary strengths to the table. My vision is that there will always be a Gold steering the ship, but you always need good people behind you, rowing.

The Small Business Administration and just about anybody else who advises small businesses will tell you that succession planning is one of the most important things for a family business to do. Luckily, I've got a great team of employees whom I'm training to support me and Seth and Ashley. When I die, I'm going to leave behind a family-run business, but it's not going to be run by my biological family alone.

One of the core members of the American Jewelry and Loan family is Brian. He runs our jewelry area, but he oversees the entire store. He was a friend of Ashley's when they were younger. I first met him when he was sixteen, and he was working as a stock clerk at Arbor Drugstore. He reminds me of me in a lot of ways. His father was a doctor; his mother was a transcriptionist. His brother is a doctor, too, and his parents wanted Brian to be a doctor as well, but he wasn't a great student. He felt that he didn't measure up. Like me, he had a lot of people telling him he wasn't going to cut it. He struggled to find a way to believe in himself. But I saw he had real potential.

We hired him to work at the store on weekends. Then, when he was nineteen and going to community college, he came to me and said, "Les, I don't think I can do this. My dad wants me to be a doctor, but I hate college." So I told him, "Here's what I can tell you. I can promise you that if you do what I tell you, you may not be a doctor or a CEO, but you will have a good life. You'll have a nice house, you'll have a nice car, you'll have a family. If you give me what I need, I promise you'll be successful. I believe that you can do this."

I've lived up to that promise, but it's because he's always done everything I've asked. Brian is a huge asset to our business. I've never for one second regretted taking that chance on him, and it's paid off for me and for him. He now has two kids, and he just bought a house two blocks away from Seth and his family. In fact, we all celebrated Hanukkah together last year. He's part of the family, and I take care of my family first.

Jeff, my jewelry repairman, is another member of the core team. He's been working with me for twenty-six years, since he was sixteen years old. His girlfriend's father was a repairman, too, and he recommended Jeff to me and suggested I bring him in through a local school program. He would go to school from nine to one, and then he'd come work for me. Jeff and I have been together longer than anyone else in the store. He's like a son to me, too. He's not only become an expert repairman, he's also recruited some of my best employees.

He's been a huge part of how we've grown this business because he gets it. He understands my vision for what a pawnshop can be. He knows the kind of person it takes to help the business grow.

Don, one of the two men who run my hard goods department (that's everything except jewelry), came to me through Jeff about fifteen years ago. He was a really good salesman, and I could see he had the aggressiveness to succeed in sales. He'd been selling electronics and guitars on the street. He's my computer person now, and between him and the other manager, Rodney, I know that whole side of the business would be in good hands if I died tomorrow.

Rodney came in when he was twenty-one years old, about twenty-three years ago. He was a hustler, too. He'd been selling jewelry on the street because at that time gold was cheap and stores would often have excess inventory they needed to move. He was aggressive, he had the drive to succeed, but out on the street he wasn't making any money. So I brought him in as my electronics salesman out in the front of the store.

Now he's one of the faces of the business—nice, smart, aggressive, great at sales. He took to pawnbroking right away. There's really no difference between hustling on the street and being a pawnbroker. We're like street hustlers in a building. Rodney's like me in that he takes the time to go around to other stores to see what things are selling for. He understands this business. Rodney is now one of four people with a set of keys to the store. I don't give out those keys to just anyone.

In building a business that will survive me, I'm not looking for one person who can do everything I do. I've had a whole lifetime to learn this business, and I'm still learning.

I'm sure there are things about the future of our business that I can't see, and that's why I'm looking to the next generation to take us to the next level. I'm building a team that together has all the skills needed to carry the business forward. And I treat everyone on that team like part of the family because love is the foundation of a family business.

Make Any Business a Family Business

Planning for the future of a business is a lot like raising kids, actually. You have to let the next generation make mistakes. That's how people learn: by screwing up, failing, and then figuring out how to pick themselves up and fix the situation. I try to give my employees the option to make mistakes.

The only way for them to get better as time goes on is to screw up.

After I die, I won't be there to bail them out. They've got to figure out how to solve problems on their own. So the balance is allowing your children or your employees to expand the business without keeping the brakes on them. You've got to bite your tongue sometimes. You've got to give them the benefit of the doubt. You've got to believe in them as much as you believe in yourself.

I'm in charge of the business and I make hundreds of decisions a day, but I try to let my kids and my employees take charge of certain areas of the business so they can experiment and learn what it's like to be in charge.

That's why Seth is in charge of our online business, which now is its own division with ten employees, bringing in about 15 percent of our revenue. He's been the one to build up that part of our business and he's made good decisions. I think it will continue to grow. Today he also runs the entire store as the COO. He's not always out on the floor, but he knows everything that's going on. It's a huge responsibility and it's wonderful for me to be able to watch him learn to run a business.

Ever since I started at American Jewelry and Loan, I've been trying to create a family atmosphere. When I started expanding the business, to every person I hired, I'd say, "Welcome to the family." To me, that means we've got one another's back through good times and bad. Back when we only had four employees, I used to bring in hot dogs for everyone on Saturday, just like my Popsie used to do at Sam's Loans. The space we're in now used to be a bowling alley, so when I first opened up in that location, on slow days we used to go in the back and bowl on the few lanes I'd kept. Then we started getting busier, so I figured, the hell with bowling. But even now that the business has gotten so much bigger, I still buy lunch a lot in December, when everybody's working long hours, or we'll have potluck lunches.

I grew up working in a family business, and I love knowing that I'm providing opportunities for my kids and my employees just the way Popsie provided a lifetime of opportunities for me. But as much as I enjoy helping the next generation succeed, I'm also grateful to everyone who comes to work for me. Especially the folks who've been with me for a long time. Because they've made a bet on me.

Some of them made that bet at a time when I had almost nothing. They took the chance that I'd be successful. Some of them, like Jeff, have been with me since the beginning and continued to believe in me, even when things looked pretty dicey. When I had to move from my fourth location in Oak Park, it was down to the very last minute before I found what is now our fifth American Jewelry and Loan store in a former bowling alley. That core group of employees believed in me. They believed I would find a new space for us. They have seen my vision, they've seen my work ethic, and they made the commitment to join my team and stay with me because of it. I am grateful for their confidence, and I want to do everything I can to repay it.

I believe that attitude helps make my business more successful. Now, I'm not exactly ready to hand over the keys, but I am making sure my core team is committed to my business for the long term, and that they're going to be taken care of for years to come. I want everyone who works for me to be able to see a path to advancement ahead of them just as clearly as they can see the way our business is going to grow. The opportunities I'm creating aren't just there for my kids, but also for anyone who's willing to work hard with our business.

In a pawnshop, you work for every single dollar. I work as hard on a $50 deal as I do on a $1,000, $10,000, or $100,000 deal. But the most important thing I can teach the next generation about this business is that it's more than dollars and cents. It's more than profit and loss. Every single deal I make, every single dollar I earn, is a dollar that's feeding my family and my employees' families. Love is a fuel that makes my business stronger. And for me, that's the beauty of a family business.

[CHAPTER 9]

Conclusion

My first trainer, the former Mr. Michigan, taught me about intensity. Whenever I started to get tired, he'd say to me, "How bad do you want it?" He'd push me to lift just a little more, go just a little further, work just a little bit harder than I thought I could. He taught me that the only difference between the person who reaches his goals and the person who doesn't is desire.

It's not enough to hope things work out the way you want. It's not enough to dream of owning your own business. It's not enough to visualize success. You've got to want it, badly. You've got to want it enough to put in the hours and make the mistakes and learn the lessons that are going to get you there. You're not going to get there unless you have the desire.

How bad do you want it?

You have to want it bad enough to face your fears. In this book I've let you see where I started out and what I had to get through to get where I am today. I hope you've learned something. I hope my story inspires you to find that desire to succeed inside yourself.

My business is changing a lot, but the core of it is always going to be the same. As I'm writing this book, in 2013, the number of loans we're making is a little bit down, but the size of those loans is up. Fewer people are pawning, but what they're pawning is more valuable. We're lending out more money on less merchandise. And redemption is flat, meaning the number of people who succeed in paying off their loans and getting their stuff back is about the same as usual. Our customers are changing, but we've still got plenty of them. I think the TV show is discouraging some customers who want anonymity from walking into our store—and I'm OK with that. While the customers are changing, the business is changing, but it's stable.

Pawnbrokers have been around for three thousand years, and three thousand years from now, we're still going to be the people's bank. We provide an essential service. People who need cash quickly, who don't have the credit history to get a more formal loan, can always come to us, and we'll give them what they need.

In fact, in some ways pawnbroking is more sustainable than banking, at least the way banks have been operating recently. Much of our economy now is based on intangibles. Banks make and lose billions on complicated bets that are about four steps removed from any actual product. A pawnbroker deals in the tangible world. My business is all about the value in objects I can see and touch. I'll pawn anything that has value—but it's got to be a real, tangible value.

I've had people come into the shop to try to pawn me an invention. I'm open-minded. I'm willing to consider it. But when I ask to see a prototype, every single time I hear, "Oh, I don't have any money to produce a prototype—that's why I'm here." Well, unlike a bank, I can't sell ideas. Bring me something I can put my hands on, something that works, and I can sell it. Otherwise we can't do business.

My life's work has been to change how people think about the service that we provide. After all, it's a simple transaction: You bring me something with real value, and I give you cash. Going to a pawnbroker doesn't have to be demeaning. The pawnshop doesn't have to be part of the world of criminals and lowlifes. These days even people who could get a loan from a bank are coming to pawnshops because they know we're ready to lend cash quickly and discreetly. I'd like to think that I've helped move the business in that direction. I'd like to think that will be part of my legacy.

Changing the image of my industry is a pretty big task. But I've never been afraid of hard work. In order to succeed, you've got to have the desire and the drive. I've got plenty of both. The only question is, how bad do *you* want it?

I started this book by talking about my father and my lifelong struggle to prove to myself that he was wrong when he said I'd never amount to anything. I showed you how I learned to face the fear he instilled in me, and how you can learn to build your own confidence so that you'll believe in your own ability to succeed. I talked about how important it is to learn to love what you do, and how you should always be pushing to keep changing and expanding your business or your career.

I also taught you how to negotiate like a pawnbroker, and I let you in on some of the secrets to building a business or career that will thrive over the long haul. I talked about how important it is to earn the trust of your community so you can build a legacy to be proud of. And I told you why I will always put family first: not just because the most successful careers are fueled by love, but because no career means anything unless it is built on a foundation of love.

I hope my story will encourage you to face your fears, risk failure, and let your fears push you forward instead of hold you back. I hope you're inspired to conquer self-doubt and find supportive voices that will help you keep striving. I hope you'll look for ways to find a passion for your work. I hope you'll always be willing to change the rules for yourself. I hope you'll find the confidence to try to negotiate. I hope that when you hit an obstacle you can't get past, you won't give up but will figure out a way to get around it. I hope you'll always pay as much attention to your reputation as you do to your bottom line. And most of all, I hope my story inspires you to see your work as something more than a way to earn a paycheck. You'll find you actually have more passion for your work when that comes second.

I believe in hard work and I believe that anyone who works hard enough can succeed. But I also believe you have to see your career for what it's worth: as a way to build a life that's always interesting, always rewarding, always challenging, and always focused on the legacy you'll leave behind you. That's what I've tried to do, and that's what I hope my story inspires you to do.

ACKNOWLEDGMENTS

Thank you to my mom for supporting me while I was growing up. To my Bubbie and Popsie for teaching me that family *always* comes first. And to Louie Kanarek for teaching me the pawnbroker shtick.

To my additional children, Stacy and Brian Lattin, who have been part of my immediate family for what seems like forever—life would most definitely be a lot less rich without you and Morgan and Harper.

Thank you to my talented and loyal American Jewelry and Loan managers, Rodney and Don, and to my gifted jeweler, Jeff. You guys have never missed a beat.

Thank you to my best friend and attorney, Mark Reizen, who is always there whenever I need him, and even when I don't know I do.

To Dr. Nick Morgan, Nikki Smith-Morgan, and Sarah Morgan, without whom this book would remain a dream gone unfulfilled.

All of my amazing friends in law enforcement hold a special place in my heart. They risk their lives every day and night so that ours can be a little richer and a lot safer. There are far too many agents, officers, commanders, and chiefs to list, yet there are a few standout stars. Jack Dalton believed in me from the beginning, helping me open American Jewelry and Loan's doors in Oak Park, Michigan, in 1978—a huge stepping-stone in the growth of the fifty-thousand-square-foot facility we have today. There are my loyal friends Ted Quisenberry, Dr. Joseph Thomas, and Haywood Julian, the last with whom I partnered to change the pawn statute in Michigan for the betterment of customers and pawnbrokers.

And of course to my amazing children, Ashley and her husband, Jordan, and Seth and his wife, Karen. They drive me every day to be the best I can be, and gave me the most incredible joy in my life: my grandchildren Evan, Madison, Brady, and Sydney.